ANGELS UNAWARES

A play, a novella, a short story

by

Dedwydd jones

First Published in 2012 by Creative Print Publishing Ltd

Paperback ISBN 978-1-909049-02-4

Creative Fiction

'Let us now praise famous men…such as have found out musical tunes.'

Ecclesiastes 1.5

The dearest friend, the kindest man, the best condition'd and unwearied spirit in doing courtesies.'

Act 3 Sc 2, The Merchant of Venice, Shakespeare.

'Let brotherly love continue. Be not forgetful to entertain strangers, for thereby some have entertained angels unawares.'

Hebrews 13,1

CONTENTS

Pic of IVOR as boy lead and glamour girl.
Photographic credits: The Rank Organisation Ltd.

CAST

David 'Ifor (Ivor) Novello' Davies,
actor-manager, composer
(age: fifteen to fifties) former student of Magdalene
College's Choir School, Oxford, principal boy soprano
soloist

Madame Clara 'Novello' Davies,
Ifor's mother, choir master, conductor
(age: thirty to seventies) domicile - Cardiff, London

David Davies,
Ifor's father, Superintendent of Rates, domicile Cardiff,
London
(age: thirty to sixties)

Bobby,
leading actor, Ifor's long-term boy friend
(age: 20 to fifties)

Eddie Marsh,
Ifor's patron, friend, civil servant, wealthy
(age: thirties to seventies)

Katie,
family friend,
(age: fifteen to thirties)

Huw ('Binkie Beaumont'), Ifor's boyfriend, business man
of the theatre
(age: nineteen to fifties)

SMALL PARTS:

Harry Tennent,
40, theatre impresario

'Dora Constable'aka **'Gladys Walton'**,
40, fan of Ifor's

Louis Mercanton,
50, film director

Judge McKenna,
magistrate

Prison Warden, 50

Prison Chaplain,
Padre Morgan, 50

Welsh Newsvendor

English Newsvendor

WALK ON PARTS:

**Tallulah Bankhead, Greta Garbo, Theatre Doorman, the Green Man, Evangeline, a singer,
Ape, a Gorilla.**

ACT 1 SCENE 1 (p 14)

Front room of spacious music studios of the Novello family, Cardiff. **Clara**, Choir Master, internationally renowned for her Royal Welsh Ladies Choir, **David**, a local Civil Servant, and **Ifor**, their son, all exceptionally gifted in music. **Clara** in triumph from recent USA tour. Discuss **Ifor's** future and family finances. **Clara** also has music salon in London. **Katie**, family friend, helps.

ACT 1 SCENE 2 (p 22)

Night. **Ifor's** rooms in Oxford. Discusses future with boyfriend **Huw**. Packs up ready to go home to Cardiff. **Huw** leaves for London.

ACT 1 SCENE 3 (p 27)

Ifor arrives home. His voice has broken. Discuss his future. **Clara** wants to go to London. **David** to stay in Cardiff in job. **Ifor** to earn living as music teacher, mainly in London.

ACT1 SCENE 4 (p 33)

Ifor's first concert in London. A disaster. Ifor upset.

ACT1 SCENE 5 (p 34)

London. Months later. Family settled in **Ifor's** flat over theatre, West End, London. **Katie** as live in helper. **Clara** disagrees with **Ifor** over his future. **Ifor's** friends, **Bobby**, and **Eddie**. **Clara** arranges tour of USA with choir, and **Ifor** as 'composer.'

ACT 1 SCENE 6 (p 41)

After USA tour. A wood. Night. Comic scene at **Clara's** artists' colony in countryside, cows and choir close by.

ACT 1 SCENE 7 (p 46)

Ifor's flat. Months later. War threatens. **Katie** helps **Ifor** start song, 'Home Fires...'

ACT 1 SCENE 8 (p 49)

Airfield. Day. **IFOR'S** pilot test flight. **Ifor's** crash

ACT 2 SCENE 4 (p 75)
Dinner with HM **Tennent**. **Ifor** invents a show on the spot. Taken up!

ACT 2 SCENE 5 (p 77)
Ivor's flat. Preparations for show, 'Glamorous Night.' A triumph. **Clara** does ad for hair shampoo. Ifor embarrassed. All cheer, laugh. Clara pretends illness. Gets her way.

ACT 2 SCENE 6 (p 83)
Ifor's flat. With **Katie**, death of **Dad** at Redroofs, **Ifor's** grief

ACT 2 SCENE 7 (p 84)
Ifor, Eddie, Bobby discuss business. **Ifor** wants to become 'actor manager' of his shows.

ACT 2 SCENE 8 (p 85)
Newsvendor reads out reviews of **Ifor's** shows.

ACT 2 SCENE 9 (p 86)
Ifor's flat. **Bobby, Ifor, Eddie** talk. **Ifor** describes meaning of his idea of theatre. Successes.

ACT 2 SCENE 10 (p 88)
Ifor's flat. **Ifor** as Henry V, fences with friends. ' **Gladys Walton** 'enters, aka ' **Dora constable**', fixes up Ifor's Rolls for petrol **Katie** enters, **Mam** dies at Redroofs. **Ifor** decides to press on.

ACT 2 SCENE 11 (p 93)
Ifor's flat. **Ifor** with **Katie,** gives her **Mam's** brooch before **Katies** leaves for Wales.

ACT 2 SCENE 12 (p 95)

Ifor's flat. Ifor receives summons to appear at Bow Street Magistrates' Court.

ACT 2 SCENE 13 (p 96)
NEWSVENDOR shouts of Ifor's arrest and arraignment. Move to Trial. Judge's summing up. Ifor sentenced to two months, one month on appeal. Taken to cells.

ACT 2 SCENE 14 (p 97)
In prison cell, Wormwood scrubs. Morning. Ifor woken up. Put to sewing up mailbags. Warder unsympathetic. Enter Padre, arranges library job and prison choir for Ifor.

ACT 2 SCENE 15 (p 102)
Ifor's flat. Ifor free again. Show doing well. Ifor to take over principal role. Gives speech of thanks on stage after show finished. Huge success.

ACT 2 SCENE 16 (p 104)
Ifor's flat. Talk of future tours, the war, concerts in France. Ifor wears his old uniform! MAGISTRATE dies. Ifor salutes him!

ACT 2 SCENE 17 (p 105)
Ifor dictates his will

ACT 2 SCENE 18 (p 106)
Ifor's *flat*. *Bobby, Eddie,* **talk of new shows. Ifor's last show. ALL toast each other.**

ACT 2 SCENE 19 (p 108)
Death of Ifor *with* Bobby *at his side. Showers of notes. NEWSVENDORS stand guard.*

ACT 1 SCENE 1

(Front room of spacious music studios of the Novello family, Cathays, Central Cardiff; Madame Clara Davies, husband David Davies, son David 'Ivor Novello' Davies; house – 'Llwyn Yr Eros,' 'Home of the Nightingales'. Late evening. Gas lights. Whole area covered with bouquets, piles of telegrams, letters, press cuttings; stacks of photos all in disorder; grand piano at back, sheet music, metronome; desk stacked with, bills, letters, photos; centre back, large model of interior of theatre; set, a court with throne; toy seats for audience; dolls in splendid uniforms, women in gorgeous costumes; wigs on stand; front of house shown with Box Office; figures up on mirror in 'foyer' are the nights' 'takings'.

In corner, phonograph, with old 'His-Master's-Voice,' trumpet, piles of records; photos of famous opera stars pinned up - Clara Butt, Angelina Patti, Christine Nilsson, Evangeline Florence, with huge pictures of scenes from grand opera; centre stage back wall, biggest photo, in large letters: 'Madame Clara Novella Davies's Royal Welsh Ladies' Choir,' with pic of CLARA holding baton in front of Ladies; at her feet, a figure, her son, IFOR, adored by Ladies; photo of IVOR, with legend, 'Boy Soprano Star of the Eisteddfod wins First Prize again!' ('Eisteddfod' - Welsh annual Festival of Music and Poetry). Various photos of 'Dancing Stones' (cromlechs); Stonehenge, stone circles, Welsh chapels, castles. Photo of MAM'S grandfather/evangelist in pulpit, Will Evans, and DAVID Davies's father, a handsome man. DAD on steps of Town Hall, Cardiff. Pic of CLARA and DAVID getting married, legend - 'Salem Chapel, Cardiff.'

Above desk, map with Welsh dragons pinned up at Cardiff, Bristol, Southampton, London. Second map of

East Coast of USA, with dragon markers at Chicago, New York, Boston, Philadelphia, CLARA'S concert Tour. Sound of cheering, applause, MADAME CLARA NOVELLA DAVIES, carrying bouquets, erupts onto stage, looks around, approaches audience, waves to them, as from royal box, throws kisses, tosses flowers. She is lavishly dressed in sweeping evening gown, with pearl necklaces, a tiara, Ostrich feather headdress, chokers, bouffant sleeves, golden shoes, with baton of gold in waist band; and the 'royal' brooch pinned on her breast; handsome, heavily made up, big bosomed, booming voice; she gives a final bow DAVID, IFOR'S DAD, a well-built, good looking, cheerful, placid, 'Superintendent of the Rates Department' at Cardiff City Hall; follows his wife, trying to restrain her. Sounds of cheers fade. DAVID tries to embrace her. CLARA pushes him off)

DAVID: It's all over now, my darling. Come to Daddy then.

CLARA: Later, you animal, my lovely! *(Of photos of choir)* see, my family, my cast, ever ready! Hello, lovely Ifor!

(CLARA 'conducts' IFOR from time to time)

CLARA: As beautiful as ever you are. Still more prizes, but listen now, I am the biggest star in this household, the first prodigy of a family of prodigies. *(Runs through voice exercises)* 'Doh, ray, mee, fah……'

DAVID: Clara, slow down!

CLARA: No!

(Opens cabinet, takes out concealed bottle of brandy, pours and drinks)

DAVID: If Ifor knew that was there, he'd chuck it into the dustbin.

CLARA: Ifor's temperance is my only disappointment in him. Anyway, I'm his mother, I drink when I want. *(Looks at cuttings, letters)* What's the news then?

DAVID *(Pours a drink):* Cheers. You swept them off their feet as usual.

CLARA: 'News' I said.

DAVID: Nice to have it all over, love?

CLARA: Don't complain - you had the seat of honour at the Reception - next to me!

DAVID: Why not, love, I am, after all, Superintendent of Rates at City Hall, am I not?

CLARA: Of course, of course…

DAVID: …it's my salary keeps the whole show going...

CLARA: … I know, I know…

DAVID: …these banquets are over soon enough, love, I'm not complaining…

CLARA: …I have always loved conquest! Like Napoleon, for me there are no Alps, just molehills. *(Drinks)* To new triumphs. Yes, I can see it, I'll have a stage set with, not one or even two, pianos, grands, of course, but with **eight** pianos, with two pianists at each keyboard, makes sixteen performers, with me holding the gold baton once again - a full stage is a full life - must make a start at once - we leave for our London 'Salon Everard' Maida Vale, on the midnight express.

DAVID: Don't be daft.

CLARA *(Of photo of Ladies with IFOR)*: How my Ladies adore Ifor.

DAVID: Your American tour was a marvel. I have to say - you did it again.

CLARA *(Dangling medal round neck):* This medal in Gold for the premiere champion Choir at Chicago's World Fair… the Ladies of South Wales! We have no hesitation,' said the adjudicators, from all over the Sates.

DAVID: Wales is proud of you.

CLARA: The world too.

DAVID: Sit down,

CLARA: I've ordered the removers to arrive momentarily!

DAVID: All the fuss, it's gone to your head.

CLARA: They give me civic receptions wherever I go now, me and my *Royal* Welsh National Ladies Choir! At Boston, New York, Southampton, Bristol, invited as guests to Osborne House, the right royal residence, Isle of Wight, and now Cardiff throws down the laurel leaves!

DAVID: All a bit too much.

CLARA: Not my fault…

DAVID: …again and again, I know, but…

CLARA: …and then the Command Performance, the whole Choir, with the royal family present! When I was presented, she said that I was lucky - to have such a handsome husband.

DAVID: You're making it up.

CLARA: I don't have to make it up. Seen your photo in the paper she had, with my Ladies, and was thrilled how we women had conquered new worlds, granted me the 'royal' for the choir, after all their work…so thrilling, this brooch… for the 'royal' Welsh choir…

DAVID: …with which you sleep every night…

CLARA: …'Victoria Regina, Imperatrix,' it says, that's the highest you can go, to the very throne! Gold enamelled in ruby red, with six diamonds. Little Clara from Tonypandy done that!

DAVID: And now she's landed back home, feet firmly on the on the ground, I hope. Here's the news. We are again near broke. *(Points at bills)* This business to sort out, bills, cheques, demands… *(Of documents)* Look, your classes, your salons, earnings, rents, expenditures… all 'losses,' here. Your telgrammes,

'Send £500 immediately.' Bills for dresses, costumes, luxury gifts, pearl necklaces…

CLARA: …imitation…

DAVID: …not what it says here. And 'wigs,' I ask you, 'Ostrich feathers, beauty parlours,' this telegram, 'Stranded in Philly. Wire one thousand at once.' 'Send cash, can't leave hotel.' And this from the last theatre, the charity performance, 'Please send remittance in name of Madame Clara. Cannot release costumes or props until bills settled.' And the takings? the profits from the tour, from our studios at Bristol, London, Cardiff, your 'salons', where are the dividends? The fees from your lessons, payments for tuition..?

CLARA: … David, my love, look at the promise in all this! Didn't George Edwardes, London's biggest impresario, just send all his Gaiety girls to me for voice training in my Everard Salon, to practice my special regimes, my tonal physicals, breath control exercises, my discovery - 'no diaphragmatic breathing' is the secret. Of course, everybody knows it now. Simple. Listen, David, understand this, never sing only with the larynx, sing with the whole body, every puff of air in your lungs, and, above all things, sing with a full heart, sing with unholy sincerity, sing with your soul in your voice, and always mean it, even if you're a bloody mouse! *(Hums scales, conducts, does breath exercises):* …doh, ray, mee, fah…

DAVID: Lovely! Calm down.

CLARA: '…soh…lah….dee…doh!' Like that! Project to the last seat in the gods! Your heart! Yes, 'God loves a cheerful giver…'

DAVID: … granddad again…

CLARA: … who was right! The good book. Forget the rest. No! Look there! *(Inspects the model theatre)* The dolls, the dolls, the wigs have been moved. He's been at it again.

DAVID: Just being himself on stage, like you said.

CLARA: Never will a son of mine go on the stage unless he is conducting grand opera. That stage there is just a passing land of make believe…'

DAVID: …don't say that in front of him.

CLARA: He dodges his opera lessons and goes to burlesques, pantos, reviews, vaudeville stuff, don't think I don't know. You must tell him, David.

DAVID: I took this recording for you, ages back. Listen to this. Exercises on piano - the piano - his other half now, a single being together - listen. *(They listen)* What is it, you ask? Exercises for ten fingers for a sixteen year old. Right? Now listen to Ifor. *(They listen)* OK. Great. Only thing is when Ifor played it, he was only FOUR years old.

CLARA: And he'll do it again and again, you'll see! Still leading boy soloist. Song and piano recitals at the Oxford Fine Arts Institute! Mother - a prodigy; son - a genius! But London's the place to conquer, Cardiff's just an empty coal shed.

DAVID: No, it is not.

CLARA: You know what I mean. My next tour…

DAVID: …I told you, no money, no tour. Look, I paid these bills out of my own savings, these…our family money, my love, is gone for the month…

CLARA: ….you're a lovely man, Dafydd, my best friend…

DAVID: …come to bed then.

CLARA: Time enough. Let's look at the bills then.

DAVID: …we've got to get an accountant, Clara. Wish Ifor was here.

CLARA: Why isn't he? He always welcomes me back. Not like him. To think of it, Dafydd, got to laugh, our beautiful Ifor arrived he did, like a wizened old goblin which I could not return, plus a conk like your Granda's, which could turn corners. But mind you, Ifor always cried in perfect thirds. And why? *(She puts phonograph trumpet over her belly)* I played this every day for one hour over my belly, from Puccini to Sullivan, to Wagner even, and 'Myfanwy' of course, with voice training added, while he was still inside me. You remember that. Our boy is a big bouncing bundle of great living Welsh music for Covent Garden itself forever from the womb, indeed!

DAVID: I'm in awe, I mean it.

CLARA: Like the rock of Gibraltar you are, love. But there is only one really big decision you ever took by yourself.

DAVID: And what was that?

CLARA: To marry me.

DAVID: Nuff said.

(They cuddle. CLARA pushes him away)

CLARA: And that nose of Ifor's, he grew into it.

DAVID: Now, these bills…

CLARA: …it is my belief that down there among our ancestors was one 'hidalgo,' that's 'aristocrat,' who fathered a child in the family at the time of the wreck of the Spanish Armada in the Irish Sea. Yes, our Ifor has romantic Mediterranean blood in his veins.

DAVID: I've got some splendid new pictures of him.

CLARA: Sorry I couldn't take him with me this time, or you either, my love.

DAVID: And the Press, they didn't forget Ifor either, the prodigy number two, who sang with the best off stage, winner of eidteddfodau!

CLARA: The ladies adore him. Sings at all my soirees here, Clara Butt, Adelina Patti, lives in Swansea now she does, good for her! - Christine Nilsson, a good start…

DAVID: …or a sad end.

CLARA: No, no…

DAVID: He's still just a boy soprano, he's lucky to have gone on as long as this.

CLARA: Off to London, I say, new challenges…

DAVID *(Points at model theatre)*: And the challenge is there. Look at that theatre. Know what? - last time I played the game with him, he charged, he did, one penny for his friends, then after the show, wrote up the takings on the mirror in the 'foyer,' there, and proceeded to buy everyone ice creams with the cash. Make it, spend it!

CLARA: Lovely. And did you put the rice pudding for him in the pantry? He likes it cold.

DAVID: Never fear. I'll put the new photos up. You wait.

(Puts up two full length photos of IFOR, one in ROBIN HOOD costume, second in MAM'S elegant Edwardian dress, IFOR looks great in both. For photos, see Sandy Wilson's, IVOR, pages 108/109)

CLARA: He's lovely there. *(Points at second pic)* and lovely there too. Dafydd, our boy, is lovely - twice! But after my dresses again, and never tidies up afterwards. Well, he did dress all the main characters, here on this stage, where he saw it all, sang it all… the Opera of Avalon, or Camelot, both in my family, and the dancing Stones up there, at Pentre Ifan, Druid enchantment…

DAVID: Clara, take it easy! Sit for a bit. Listen, his second prize at college was for arithmetic.

CLARA: And French.

DAVID: He's learned to count, thank goodness, which is more that can be said for his amazing Mam. Now, here's more bills, wait a minute. (Sees ltters) Damn, didn't see these… *(Tears open a letter)*

CLARA: …what is it?

DAVID:…from Ifor! *(Slumps. Looks at CLARA)*

CLARA *(understands):* We can't go to London now.

DAVID: No.

CLARA: My poor lovely boy. Where is he?

DAVID *(Reading letter):* 'Train in the morning.' Signs off, 'your fallen star…'

CLARA: …no son of mine's ever going to be that!

DAVID: But what can he do now? His scholarship is finished. A miracle it lasted as long. It's all right, love. I'll put on 'Myfanwy.' *(A famous Welsh song sung by boy soprano. They look at the photos of IFOR, arms round each other, lights, fade Myfanwy, dim lights. SPOT on NEWSVENDOR side stage front, strolls on)*

NEWSVENDOR: Read all about it. Read all about it! Good old Clara, gold medal for Wales. World Champion! Queen of the Royal Box! Mother of our Ifor! And Ifor wins eisteddfod gold again! Mam and son, what a double! There's lovely! Read all about it!

(Strolls off stage. CUT LIGHTS)

ACT 1 SCENE 2

(Night. IVOR'S room in Magdalene College Choir School, Oxford. IVOR, and HUW, IFOR'S BOYFRIEND. HUW'S suitcase by door. Books in neat piles. Upright piano. Stacks of sheet music. IFOR in student gown. On shelf, IFOR'S mortar bard, by bowl of fruit, coins, bank notes. IFOR pauses, looks down at his body)

IFOR: Huw, my body is not the same as it was yesterday.

HUW: You'll get used to it.

IFOR: I don't sing, I just croak like a tired old bullfrog. Star at the eisteddfod, star here in Oxford, star at Cardiff, star with the Ladies, star with the stars. And now, star nowhere.

HUW: Star at the keyboard, Ivor, star at the melodies. Heard you yesterday and today, it hasn't changed! You are one great lovely tune yourself.

IFOR: A friend of friends, Huw.

(They embrace. IFOR decides)

IFOR: You're right, I must get used to it. Boy sopranos don't last forever.

HUW: You've had a good run, I mean, you're just sixteen, and the old bollocks only dropped yesterday.

IFOR: Yours are still friendly enough. What am I going to do?

HUW: Do your parents know?

IFOR: I wrote them.

HUW: Not going to stay in Cardiff, are you?

IFOR: No idea. Mam won't. Says Wales is a neglected old empty old coal shed.

HUW: Or an old empty chapel. What happens In Wales? Nothing, not even hope. London's the place. I was a call-boy at the Prince of Wales down there by the station, Cardiff, for two years. Nothing Welsh about it. Then here at the Playhouse, almost London. At least you know what's going on. You got a good taste of it here too. My Dad was right. Accountancy or undertaking. Adding up or putting down! So it's numbers for me. You know my Pa, who is my Pa, by the way, I'll let you into a secret, Francis, of Francis and Jones, timber merchants, I am his bastard. But he's backing me! How about that!? Contracts, box office, profit and loss, auditioning, costings, how to run a business, how to handle cash, as long as his bastard is not in Cardiff. OK with me, fine with him. Get on like a house on fire. I'm going - palaces. You watch!

IFOR: And who do you know in London?

HUW: A man who never gives up.

IFOR: That makes two of us. *(THEY embrace)* Don't forget the accent, learned mine back stage from the actors.

IFOR: Not the only thing you learned.

HUW: I'm still with you, aren't I?

IFOR *(In posh accent):* What a splendid chap you are.

HUW *(Posh accent):* I say old fella, you're quite right.

IFOR: Don't think I'll bother. It's the accent of melody that enraptures me.

HUW: If you've got the right social accent, you get served faster. Really. It's the accent that means 'well-connected,' 'old boy net,' and it works.

IFOR: Crude verbally as I am, I'm sure they'll accept my poor little talents.

HUW: Like all your Mam's lovely ladies.

IFOR: And her lovely gentlemen too! Here. Before you go, have these*. (Puts coins, bank notes, fruit into mortar board)* From my fans yesterday, at my last concert, Winnie, Dilys, Dorothy, swore they'd follow me to London. Gave them all a hug. There's lovely. You can have my mortar board too. My gown I shall leave for the next occupant. Take the cash. That's it. Off to Cardiff, 'home of Nightingales' tomorrow. And Huw, I can manage. Always give lessons, concerts, as an accompanist now. Got all my stuff...*(Hands him mortar board, full of goodies)*

HUW: Ta *(They kiss)* What about your songs?

(Ifor picks up pile of music mss)

IFOR: Here, my recent efforts, knew I had to do something before my voice – 'drooped.' Came up with this – *The Fickle Jade,* a musical show, with songs for everyone. Even a walz on ice. Ten copies I sent out. Responses? - two copies lost forever, the rest, ballads, dance numbers, review tunes, burlesques, plus pastoral content, rejected. Never a star will I be in Tin Pan Alley, and company.

HUW: And what are you going to do about it?

IFOR: As soon as I get to Cardiff, I intend to write a half a dozen more.

HUW: That's my boyo! You got the touch, the gift, I can sense it. I been meaning to ask, Ifor, why'd you take those manuscripts or those dolls, and even that old tea cosy, to bed with you?

IFOR: To keep them warm. Everything has feelings. I've even warmed up a pair of book-ends in bed, and they were so grateful. All the things of the world need comfort, friendship, that's why this place had been so happy for me, I've made so many friends, in bed and out of it! And it's not true what these rejections say about my songs, 'crude and unorchestrated.' People want tunes, not hundreds of instruments without one. Who can hum a tuba when they leave the theatre? So from now on, it's tunes, tunes all the way. I think I'll write a musical show based on the Tonypandy eisteddfod, 'Lily of the Valley?' What do you think?

HUW: Depends on the lilies.

IFOR: Mam said I must 'never be afraid to show the soul in my voice,' like my Granddad the Preacher.

HUW: Your Mam's right.

IFOR: These breathing exercises of hers, they're famous now.

HUW: Follow your Mam then.

IFOR: But she's a terrible spender, and a bit of a boozer.

HUW: She's famous and loved, too, all over Wales.

IFOR: My granddad named her 'Novello' after that Italian soprano of his youth…

HUW: …and she never looked back.

IFAN: They've been so good to me here…

HUW: …in a divine English College of music.

IFOR: Darling!

HUW: And you to them too. You doubled their Sunday concert audiences.

IFOR: But, one thing I've learned, Huw, how much I've got to learn. Almost frightening.

HUW: Like your Mam said, 'do the 'quarry-face' work, everyday at the piano, and one day you'll wake up and find you've built a castle!' You feel better now?

IFOR: Getting used to it, like you said. I love giving the little talent I have to others, to the audiences, to friends and all. I can feel the enjoyment welling up from the stalls, till it fills the whole auditorium. It isn't just the giving - that would be selfish - it's the sharing. I shall miss that.

HUW: More songs, Ivor.

IFOR: Perhaps I should send some to the boulevard theatres of gay Paris. I could translate them myself. This little beat-up piano tells more of the truth than I ever could. *(Plays)* Hear? It's the little finger. See the lump on the second joint, chronic. Born with it. Can't straighten it, ossified cartilage. Can never be a pianist, just an accompanist.

HUW: You got songs dropping off every other finger, ifor, it's only one finger versus nine. Bloody good odds, I'd say.

IFOR: I can't sing any longer.

HUW: Listen to the music, you've got it all at your finger tips, honest! There there.

IFOR: Thanks, Huw. I swear I'll never be a failure again.

HUW: You never were! *(They embrace)* That's the spirit! Better be off now, boyo.

IFOR *(Of presents):* Put them in your suitcase. *(HUW sweeps IFOR'S presents into his suitcase)* Take the mortar board too. I have no need of it now. Honest. Give it to your Dad.

HUW: I will, too!

IFOR: You'll be busy, I understand. Try to keep in touch.

HUW: That's OK, bye, bye for now, my most marvellous music lover! *(Shouts off)* And goodbye, Dad, from your favourite bastard!

(EXIT HUW. IFOR slumps on bed, head in hands. He goes over to piano, plays a few bars, LIGHTS FADE as IFOR plays with greater and greater passion. CUT LIGHTS, SOUND)

ACT 1 SCENE 3

(Late morning. Front room Studios, Cardiff, as before. Books, music etc, tidied up. KATIE, daughter of one of CLARA'S singers, helps. Trunks and suitcases packed. DAVID sitting, reading music. CLARA, pacing, dressed magnificently.)

KATIE: My Mam says she's never enjoyed herself so much in her life!

CLARA: She's our best contralto, Katie, so she must be right! Just about finished. Here's your wages, go on, take it.

KATIE: I'll miss you both.

DAVID: Now there goes a rare spirit, bless her.

(KATIE hugs them. EXIT KATIE. CLARA gazes at pictures of IFOR on wall)

CLARA *(murmurs)*: Luvly!

DAVID: What do I say about all this to Ivor?

CLARA: Don't 'say,' just 'do,' give him a kiss, a hug.

DAVID: It's a delicate matter.

CLARA: No man's bollocks are 'delicate!'

DAVID: He'll want to take his theatre with him.

CLARA: We don't know if he's going first.

DAVID: Last night here – or the first? Come on, Ifor. Wonder what he'll sound like.

CLARA: Whatever he sounds like, it will be exactly like Ifor, our dear boy, alright? I'll give him some of my secret vocal exercises so he'll sound even sweeter, whatever.

DAVID: Nothing any of us can do about it, this time, even you Clara, it's human biology.

CLARA: Human testiclees!

(Knock on at front door)

CLARA: He's here.

(ENTER IFOR, with suitcase. Embraces them. IFOR tries to speak, shrugs, bursts into tears. CLARA and DAD comfort him)

IFOR *(croaking):* I'm…so…sooo… very sorrry…never be 'normal' again, Doc said, whatever 'normal' means. Those photos…

DAVID: …lovely they are.

CLARA: Just put the dresses back in the wardrobe next time, ifor.

IFOR: Sorry, Mam.

DAVID: What about…?

IFOR: … singing? I don't know. I'm like an old bull frog at the moment. Feel I've let you down, college, the eisteddfod, here, Cardiff, us, the family…

CLARA: …now you listen, you've let nobody down. Simply because your balls, guided by biology, as your father says, have had to 'readjust' themselves - I can say that, I'm your Mam - this does not represent betrayal of anyone, except yourself, and only if you let it, which you will not. A second life is what you've been offered. Remember that! No failure there at all.

IFOR: Ta, Mam. Gave away my gown and mortar board. Had a last concert at in the College hall. How they all cheered. They knew I was…breaking, and still they cheered. Never let me down, no, never. Huw was there and the girls, Winnie and my friends...

DAVID: ...you see, Ifor, another triumph.

IFOR: It was just my turn to give, that's all. But My *'Fickle Jade'* songs were all rejected.

DAVID: So? *(Gets pile of blank sheet music)* Get on with more.

CLARA: *(Of model)* And don't look at the theatre, Ifor.

IFOR: It's just a model.

CLARA: The theatre is a place of pretence...

IFOR: ...and acting...

CLARA: ...just make believe.

IFOR: I agree. Lovely spot!

CLARA: Not lovely, ifor! Lies, deceit! Stick to Opera. Some truth there!

DAVID: We been doing some talking and thinking about our new plans...

CLARA: ...first, we're going to London, Dad's located another salon...

IFOR: ...how much is it going to cost?

DAVID: ...don't worry, fully paid up. Enough room for us all, and our students, and Mam's Ladies.

CLARA: And look, the dolls, theatre, metronome, photos, the phonograph, and the new slide machine. Everything ready to go with you, anything you can hug. Decide what to do later. Just fixed up a charity show with my Choir this morning, with my friend Evangeline, in London. As for your song...

IFOR: ...my song?! They rejected it.

CLARA: Not when I visited them.

IFOR: Mam! You didn't...!

CLARA: I am the professional in this house.

IFOR: ...but my voice...

CLARA: ...not singing ...you'll be the accompanist...

IFOR: ...yes, second string now.

CLARA: Nothing of mine will ever be 'second string,' especially my son!

IFOR: Mam, you're lovely when you're in full flood.

CLARA: Of course I am, and what's more important, I know what to do with it! Now that little song of yours…

IFOR: …'Spring of the Year'….

CLARA: Evangeline will premiere it.

IFOR: Mam, you sure?!

DAVID: 'Composer, accompanist,' Ifor, sounds a bit better than just 'singer', or 'actor.' And…and tell him, David.

CLARA: No. You do.

DAVID: Mam's got her next big project planned.

CLARA: I've been in touch with my Ladies. Strike when the iron is hot!

IFOR: What's the plan?

CLARA: A Romany Arts Colony in the open countryside!

IFOR: Terrific. I've always wanted to be a gypsy boy! What about Ruritania?

DAVID: No, Ifor. That is in the dream stage.

CLARA: Mine first, Ifor, I'm your Mam, remember.

IFOR: Of course, of course.

CLARA: And apart from the Gypsy arts encampment - just talked to Evangeline, she's got a friend moving out of her flat. And guess where that flat is? Over the roof of the Vaudeville Theatre, on the Strand, even a sun terrace with it…

IFOR: …but I been there to see George Edwardes…the Gaiety is just opposite…

CLARA: …those revue shows, cloud cuckoo land, not a note of truth among the lot of them. Well, I've taken the flat for us, Dad arranged the deposit, and for you really, Ifor, your sounding board, your second life, big enough for all of a family.

IFOR: Such great news. *(Embraces her)* But Dad, you are coming, aren't you?

DAVID: I'll be visiting weekends for now. Don't worry, I'll be here and there, enjoying both your successes, that's what I was put on this earth for, alright, I am your best audience. So no fears, Ifor, we'll come in first, together.

IFOR: Well, look, I been working part time with Huw, at the Oxford Playhouse, front of house, saved some money, and I can teach piano too, always turn in a penny or two, I promise, Huw put me onto it. Here, here's ten pounds, just help getting started …

CLARA: …you luvely boy!I

DAVID: Well done, Ifor!

CLARA: But this is not the end of 'Llwyn yr Eros,' I promise you. And David will still be here, here serving the Muse of Song for us!

IFOR: When do we leave?

CLARA: The removals came this morning and went this morning. Last van, later this afternoon. I've arranged for porters and cleaners. Katie will keep n eye on the place. We leave on the evening express. The flat will be ready for us and the new Salon will be overrun with Welsh Ladies.

IFOR: One day what about a show based on the capital of Glamor, Camelot!

DAVID: You calm down now. Can't have Camelot, anyway, too expensive.

IFOR: Curtain up! Curtain up! Tickets, please. Thank you, thank you *(Mimes taking money)* And now time for ice cream again, and the rest for Mam. *(Mimes giving money to CLARA)*

CLARA: No, keep it. Write more songs for you fans.

IFOR: Where do I find fans now?

CLARA: People the halls with nobles of the imagination, Ifor. That's what I do!

IFOR: I'll work out the next bit when I come to it.

DAVID: That's more like it.

CLARA: This is not the end of the 'Home of the Nightingale,' just the beginning!

IFOR: Bless Madame Clara Novello, my musical guide and mentor, my muse, never been able to say 'no' to her'! You see, she sort of sorts out the scales from the fluff, so to speak, like a clearing vision behind my eyes. Like I'm playing for her and I look up. In the centre of the room, close to the ceiling I make out a wide-winged white albatross-bird hovering over the piano. As I watch, it grows like into a great spreading cloud, then it dissolves, shedding its feathers one by one, and they all float downwards, a slow, silent fluttering of many plumes. Then as I play on, they begin to quiver and dance in my eyes, and change into notes themselves, quavers, semi quavers, untold groupings till the whole ceiling looks like moving layers of fluttering white musical notes in a breeze. Then the feather notes fall free, come to rest on my tinkling fingers and irresistibly urge them on, a miracle! - in fitting multitudinous arrangements, every one, till I see the whole notes of the song laid out on the keys in one long melodious line. Then I write it down. And where is she now, you ask, my muse and her serviteurs? Why, all flown home to here, to prepare for the next festival of light here for her son and lumiere, in the theatre avenues of London. Bless you, Mam.

MAM: After all that codswallop, Ifor, you shall have a grand piano in your flat, It's about the only thing that understands what you're talking about.

DAVID: The Ladies follow their Muse too!

CLARA: And before you go, there's fresh rice pudding in the pantry.

IFOR: Love you both! *(To the rooms and pictures)* So, hail and farewell, my nightingalesl! … *(Clears throat)* Don't worry. My second life starts here and now All will be well as long as I don't sing. Now, with Myfanwy, round about Camelot.

CLARA: Yes, nice and peaceful.

(Arms round each other, they gently sing passages of 'Myfanwy.' The two 'Wilson' photographs of IFOR centre background. Fade lights, singing)

ACT 1 SCENE 4

(Sound of audience murmuring, coughing. Piano tinkling softly. Spot on IFOR side stage, at piano. Spot on CLARA off side stage, motioning to IFOR. Soprano EVANGELINE makes two false starts, finally jumps in, finishes song. Spattering of applause. EVANGELINE flounces off past IFOR, wags her finger. IFOR about to rush off, CLARA catches him by the arm)

CLARA: Well, my boy!?

IFOR: Mam, done it again.

CLARA: Done what?

IFOR: Evangeline! Mam, she said she couldn't hear my notes.

CLARA: So Evangeline couldn't hear her cues.

IFOR: She should have told me.

CLARA: She did. *(Wags finger)* Like that.

IFOR: What did I do wrong?

CLARA: You knew the music, you knew the words, you knew the singer, you knew the audience, but you didn't know the acoustics. So, what did you do wrong?

IFOR: I didn't hold a sound rehearsal.

CLARA: That's it.

IFOR: And you told me to hold one.

CLARA: I didn't just say 'I told you so.'.

IFOR: Failed again.

CLARA: Stop it! Never use that word again! Listen! For a professional, it's never a failure, just a learning curve. Not a success, not a flop; a postponement, not a cancellation. You got your name on the music circuit, a name check with a good singer, at a top venue, high profile anyway. And now you're hurting, so you're a professional too. Welcome! Just remember one thing, 'Persistence is of the essence!' as the good book says.

IFOR: Mam, what would I do without you?

CLARA: You'd live, and love your life, like me.

IFOR: Why do they say Dad hasn't got an enemy in the world?

CLARA: I won't hear a word against your father, alright?

IFOR: Sorry, Mam…I…

CLARA: And now, off to our new home.

IFOR: What for me now?

CLARA: You're s musician, aren't you?

IFOR: Well, yes.

CLARA: A professional?

IFOR: Yes, that's it!

CLARA: Then make music!

(EXIT IFOR, CLARA, arm in arm)

ACT 1 SCENE 5

(Months later. The NOVELLO's spacious flat, the Strand, West End, London, situated at top of Vaudeville Theatre, a terrace looking out over the Strand, and river. Traffic sounds, horns, church bells, shouts, flapping of pigeons. Shut windows to cut off sound. Living room. Fittings all in white, white panels, ceiling, doors, grand piano, carpet, with brass fittings, vases of marble, alabaster light stands, ash trays, objets d'art, in

white stone and marble. Centre stage, grand piano, in white. Furnishings, sofa, chairs also in white. The two 'Wilson' photos of IFOR, up. Metronome. Box with screen and slides. Phonograph. Old trumpet hangs on wall. False bookshelves conceal IFOR'S records. Cocktail cabinet with bottles. Model of theatre centre back. Entrance to flat offstage left through doorway. Off too are CLARA'S rooms. Off right, IFOR's bedroom. Up back centre a French window, with sun terrace outside, spectacular view of Strand, the Gaiety, and silhouette of London rooftops. Pics of Cardiff, his old home, Prince of Wales Theatre (Cardiff), cromlechs, Stonehenge, CLARA's Choir, (with 40 Ladies!) various cuttings, posters. Desk with piles of letters and mss of songs. IFOR is searching, looking for lost letter)

IFOR: Mam! Mam! *(Goes to entrance)* Mam! *(He searches. ENTER CLARA, dressed for going out)*

IFOR: What a mess it all is in here.

CLARA: Katie will clear it up.

IFOR: How is she today?

CLARA: Feel responsible. After she left us in Cardiff - robbed, abused, beaten to a pulp. On her way from school. Imagine. In Cathays. Couldn't speak for weeks. Doctor advised complete change. Imagine that, at fifteen. What a start in life.

IFOR: Thank goodness we've got a spare room downstairs. Katie is one of us already.

CLARA: You're a lovely boy. Katie thinks so too.

IFOR: Yes, Mam, you're right, 'what a start.'

CLARA *(Conducts):* Just off to rehearsal with my Ladies.

IFOR: Mam, wait. Have you seen a letter - from the Adelphi Theatre.

CLARA: Well, it might have got delivered late…

IFOR: … Mam, I got the part. That letter was to confirm it, with times of rehearsals…

CLARA: …no son of mine is going to be a mere spear-carrier or call boy!

IFOR: It was the lead. I was the Count of Luxembourg!

CLARA: What kind of nonsense is that?

IFOR: You took that letter, didn't you?

CLARA: You are a great opera composer. Don't turn your back on that grand destiny.

IFOR: OK, Mam, go to your rehearsal. Go On. Conduct. Sing. I can't.

CLARA: We all love you, Ifor.

IFOR: Only way I can get on a stage is to act!

CLARA: Don't even think of it! There, my boy, 'hope maketh not ashamed.' you'll see. And you would like to come with us to Canada, this time, New York later, again, with the Ladies, wouldn't you?

IFOR: …America?! …bit of a dream, Mam?

CLARA: I am the Mam that makes dreams come true.

IFOR: Well, you certainly fooled me. Just joking.

CLARA: I should hope so. And I've still got plans for that big gypsy camp, too.

IFOR: What did you think of Eddie Marsh - last night?

CLARA: Liked him best of all, I think. A good heart. And he's on your side, like me, like the family, like all of us.

IFOR: He's Winston Churchill's private secretary.

CLARA: I'm sure he is, love.

IFOR: Eton and Oxford.

CLARA: You are Oxford too, but you are remembered!

IFOR: Eddie is immensely wealthy.

CLARA: Very sensible. I'm glad you met him. You're over your 'Song of Spring' with Evangeline now, so get on with the next one! Well, off I go!

IFOR: And leave the front door open for Bobby.

CLARA: I like your Bobby too, he's never afraid to answer back.

IFOR: He is also a first class West End actor.

CLARA: Enough of this 'West End' stuff. There is only one theatre in the West End worth the candle, and that is Covent Garden!

(EXIT CLARA. IFOR searches. EXITS to CLARA'S room. ENTER BOBBY, IFOR'S boyfriend. IFOR RE-ENTERS waving letter)

IFOR: In her dressing room table. See, I told you, she hid it.

BOBBY: She's not trying to put you down, Ifor.

IFOR: No, she's not. She's trying to put me up, only I don't like the way she's going about it. See this letter? I got it, as accompanist, and walk on, I did not fail. Accompanist and actor! Says, since I didn't turn up for rehearsal, they assumed I'd turned down the part.

BOBBY: You're writing songs morning, noon and night. Piles of them there. 'Why Hurry Little River?' 'Bravo Bristol, 'In the Clouds' here, liked that one, and your 'Skating Walz,' music is tops, I'm sure that one would be a hit. Concentrate on that.

IFOR: Today, tomorrow, as you say, 'concentrate.'

BOBBY: I sent a whole collection of your songs out to various publishers, all good stuff, but ...

IFOR: …thanks so much, my love, but I feel… I've got so far to go. *(Of letters)* Help seal up this lot, Bobby, wake up the fools! Post office is ready, just opposite!

BOBBY: What about this American trip you mentioned?

IFOR: Not America. Canada this time, mainly. Stopping off at New York. Mam's old friends from her first tours. To celebrate the British Empire! Yanks don't agree! Imagine. I shall accompany a song or two of my own, too, Mam's seen to that. This time everyone will hear me. Mam's a star in her own right, after all. Look at this, from a critic.

BOBBY *(reading, parodying):* 'We theatre artists, we write and act to please the people, to fill the plush, to convey our emotions across the footlights so they can share in our rhapsodies.'

IFOR: Don't use language like that in front of Mam, or you won't last a second, Bobby. But, yes, that's about it, but you only have to do it, not teach it. Mam thinks 'stage' is all pretence. Music is the eternal white triumph of our imaginings, and never fades, and only in opera. And look down there, across the road, you can see the Gaiety Theatre and George Edwards's last burlesque shows. Now it's our turn, I hope! How's it going, you ask? For a start, they've rejected my re-written *The Fickle Jade*. En masse. Theatre Managers from one end of the street to the other.

BOBBY: Well, they're going to look very silly one day. Eddie Marsh is spending his entire inheritance backing young men of talent, real talent, like Rupert Brooke, Siegrid Sassoon last night. Like you. Very clever boys, and some big talents.

IFOR: What are you then, my Bobby?

BOBBY: I am the great deliverer of the talented and a fine actor in my own right. You'll do splendidly, any day now really, you're so beautiful.

IFOR: Come off it, Bobby.

BOBBY: Everyone's saying it. Even the girls.

IFOR: Especially the girls.

BOBBY: Your future army of fans is just warming up!

IFOR: You jealous?

BOBBY: Only when we're apart.

IFOR: Then we must stay together.

BOBBY: But you will be a star one day. I mean, that profile, that piano...

IFOR: …OK, OK…

BOBBY: Don't you ever write down the notes, your words, Ifor?

IFOR: No, I just remember them, one at a time, while I'm working on the next in my head, much easier.

BOBBY: Mahler, Ravel, Debussy, you played them all till midnight. How do you do it?

IFOR: I learned them. In the womb. It's just memory, Bobby, just a trick of nature. Like French. Learned it in a term. *(Points at trumpet)* The songs come through that trumpet direct from Avallon. And in spite of my conk, a 'star' you say? Of stage? Mam would rather cut my legs off. A l'attaque! Post these, Bobby? Must be some hope out there.

BOBBY: Sure.

(EXIT BOBBY, with letters. IFOR addresses more envelopes. CLARA erupts, waving letters)

CLARA: Forget those! Our tour budgets are approved. We go, the whole Choir, for the Festival of Empire, Montreal, Toronto…. A pageant! Red coat reconstruction battle scenes, choruses of Redskins, pioneers in canoes, Indian scouts. *(Waves docs)* to celebrate HER! *(Indicates her 'royal' brooch)* 'Imperatrix.' All here. And you, my young champion are going too, and you are going as I planned, as the sole official **Composer**. You will write all the music for it! And play it, as accompanist, and loudly enough this time! Contracts here! And it will all be an outstanding success, again and again!

IFOR: All the music, mine? Does it really say that?

CLARA: No such thing as a mountain for your Mam. And you will meet all the stars of the Opera in New York, and play for them to, hear the very words of 'The Magic Flute', at last! And meet Hollywood celebrities, too.

IFOR: All strangers to me, Mam.

CLARA: 'Be not forgetful to entertain strangers,' Ifor, 'for thereby some have entertained angels unawares…'
IFOR: …hang on a bit…
CLARA: …if you dropped dead tomorrow, the world would never have heard of you, so get up, go, go, except for the 'Home Fires', got to finish it, you've got some songs there, I've looked through them, they'll do for a start. But finish 'Fires.' I know it would work. And we'll do 'Song of Spring' too' and this time, with a sound rehearsal!
IFOR: Is Evangeline still talking to me?
CLARA: Of course. She's had 'embarrassments' like that too. She's fine. You wait. And now it's for 'Empire' and 'Imperatrix'! Magic words, which I wear on my bosom even now. And Katie's better already. Settling in fine. Thank you, my boy! You help her.
IFOR: I just talk to her.
CLARA: Exactly.
(RE-ENTER BOBBY)
IFOR *(Of CLARA):* Look at her, isn't she beautiful today! Her face, like the Archangel Gabriel herself, and she bears good tidings too. I'm off, Bobby, the Empire trip!
BOBBY: That jamboree, is it? Do it much better at the Chrystal Palace, with myself in the lead, of course. And don't forget to drop in on those new Hollywood studios, too.
IFOR: I can see it now! Quebec, the death of Wolfe. Birth of a nation!
CLARA: So you did know about the trip, my little Welsh weasel!
IFOR: Half your mail for the last two months had been from Canada and the US, Mam.

CLARA: Bobby. Last night, with those amazing young men, it was, how shall I put it, magical. I felt I was in Fairyland!
(IFOR and BOBBY roar with laughter. Put arms round CLARA)
IFOR: We all love you, too!
(FADE LIGHTS, SOUND OF TRAFFIC)

ACT 1 SCENE 6
(MONTHS later. Warm summer night. Pathway in countryside. Wind in trees. Owls hoot. Moonlight on and off, behind clouds. CLARA in finery, parasol, with IFOR. Both pause breathless)
IFOR: We're in the middle of a wood now, Mam.
CLARA: I promised you a surprise.
IFOR: After New York and the new world, I suppose I'll have to go along with it. What have you cooked up this time? *(CLARA strides ahead)* Mam, where are you taking me?
CLARA: You'll see.
IFOR: Our boat only came the day before yesterday, so give us a rest.
CLARA: Memorable! Yes, in New York, that party I gave, only for blacks. That gave those palefaces an idea of what's it's like to be discriminated against! Then I thought, a party for whites only, but the only song of the evening I gave to a black singer and she sang 'Cherry Ripe' all night. Memorable! And you remember the appeal I organised with the help of the Mayor of New York himself, for musical instruments to send to the dough boys when they go overseas! Thousands came in, from French horns to penny whistles. They will rise like a ghostly orchestra over the winds of Flanders field. All that, my doing. Check with the Mayor! So be patient. Madame Clara always delivers! I thought the

41

Southampton reception wasn't up to it, didn't you? Not half enough bouquets for my Ladies.

IFOR: Another triumph, Mam, and you looked grand as usual.

CLARA: Lovely boy. But I'll have a word with the Mayor. A banquet next time.

IFOR: We are now on top of a hill, still in the middle of a wood. Are you happy with this outcome, Mam?

CLARA: Moon is out again.

IFOR: Where on earth are we going to sleep tonight?

CLARA: My goodness, just look at that bush, and that one, why there are a lot of bushes all round.

IFOR: Mam, what are you talking about?

(CLARA drags a travelling trunk from behind a bush)

CLARA: Well, look what I found*! (Drags out 'Druid' costumes, floral wreathes, bunches of flowers. Dances about, humming, conducting her Ladies, in the bushes, runs through voice exercises)* That's it, yes, slower. Face this way! He's here! Take a bow, Ifor, we were all waiting for you. *(Sound of applause, fades)* Carry on Ladies. And don't worry, Ifor, their nourishment is provided for around here, by the farm down there, cows, fresh eggs, new butter, cooking over wood fires, fresh cream from the dairy. I am convinced the cows give more milk when we sing to them, they love Mozart, but Puccini is best. Never seen so much milk the locals say, and the gypsies too, say I have established a most unusual harmony between them, nature and the locals. Everyone is happy, you see, and healthy! Wait till you see the cows at milking, they're practically dancing too! Ifor, this is our new commune, a pastoral artists' community in the middle of lots of vegetation! The caravans too, all colours of the rainbow. And after all this heaven, our dear old Dad waiting at home to welcome us too!

IFOR: These hills would have been a bit too strenuous for him, I think.

CLARA: Not for your Mam, though! Hello, every one of you lovely invisible ladies! *(Cheers from LADIES)*

IFOR: It is amazing. But have you got permission?

MAM: We bring in a lot of business for the locals, our ladies have healthy appetites and even healthier after they've been here a day or two. We will rehearse practically every opera that's ever been written, right here in the bushes. Under the undergrowth, in sunshine and rain, and all on these new phonograph records. *(Cheers from shadows)* Everybody is so friendly in the fresh air.

IFOR: Lovely, Mam, really. How did you…?

MAM: …all in place before we left, had to do something, didn't I, for when I came back? My new colony, artists only allowed. *(Shouts instructions)* Come on out, we're here. And the breathing, from the whole body, you puffing young things. Come on. Do, ray, me, fah…*(She hums loudly, conducting the shadows. Owls hoot.)* Speak up, speak up *(Sound of aria from 'The magic Flute.' MAM seizes IFOR, dances with him)*

CLARA: The Magic Flute is always better in the open air.

IFOR: Mam, stop it, you are exhausting me, however lovely…

CLARA: …look over there. See those flashes. That's photography. There and there. Photos all over, in The Tatler, they love my 'exotic flourishes,' as they call them. I am good copy wherever I go. And I've got gypsy wagons drawn up in the clearing, and two from the local Romany caravans, authentic. We tell the time, we sing, we dance the ancient pastoral dances of the antique tribes. But notice my motions, my elegant movements, my poses for my ladies at all times of the day and for you one day too, the acme of elegance. You're a bit skinny, ifor, but you've got the right height. (*Shouts off*) It's warm tonight, Ladies, so bring out your sleeping bags! We sleep under the leaves, and above them, the stars! See, my Ladies waving from the underbrush! Already they blossom like flowers, put that in the copy, Tatler! They have been re-born already! They are more and more supple in limb, more graceful in gesture, the livelong day; their voices rounded, and their spirits free as the very roots wherever they grow. And here, another little surprise! *(Gives documents to IFOR)* Look at those, and dance with the cows! All your songs! Your Mam only deals with success, there, there, best publishers in town! See, what happens when your Mam gets a grip on your future. They want you to write whole shows, although they rejected the 'Fickle Jade,' the hypocrites. Before I left, I called on each of them, and I warned them, face to face, that if you were not given your due by the time I was back, I'd call on them every day, hammer on their doors, until they saw the light and declared your genius to the world! My son, Ivor Novello, offspring of another genius, Madame Clara Novello Davies!…

IFOR: …I'm quite out of breath again, Mam.

CLARA: …and even this new 'Rat' of yours too, your dirtiest play, even though I hate the nasty little rodents, I read it, I think it might work.

IFOR: How'd you mean?

CLARA: Eddie's backing it too.

IFOR: Wonderful! Give me time to think!

CLARA: Come on now. *(She takes out lady's gypsy costume for Ifor)* Stand still. Now… *(Ifor peers at documents. She dresses IFOR)* There! You are a Princess of the old Romany communes…

IFOR: … in love with the Prince of the line who is imprisoned by his vicious old horse-thief guardian of an uncle, the Prime Minister, am I right?

(IFOR sits, laughing. Flash photo of IFOR)

CLARA *(Shouts off)*: And make sure that that photo gets in your main columns too – Ivor Novello, my son, fresh back from triumphs in the USA, like me!

(Figure detaches itself from the shadows. It is the mythological 'Green Man, decked out with leaves, like the branches of a tree. He capers. IFOR, MAM jump in surprise. ALL laugh. FADE GREEN MAN).

IFOR: Who… on earth was that? Was that you?

MAM: Not me! But I recognise him from the Vale of Glamor, the Green Man, Ifor, protector of forests, creator of floral dances and inspirer of folk songs! He appears only when he wishes to bless man's endeavours - mine, in this case!

IFOR: If you say so, Mam.

(IFOR waves. cheers from Ladies, camera flashes. As Ladies sing, heads (cut outs) of cows appear over bushes, swaying to music, begin to moo in time. MAM conducts, IFOR gazes in awe)

CLARA: That was the Ladies.

IFOR: That was the cows.

CLARA: The Ladies!

IFOR: The cows, you mean?

CLARA: No. The Ladies I mean.

IFOR: The ladies are cows.

CLARA: No, they are not.

IFOR: Have it your way, Mam.

CLARA: Of course, love. The loveliest body of voices in the world!

(Ladies sing in moonlight, mooing along with cows, CLARA and IFOR, dance to chorus of songs and moos)

ACT 1 SCENE 7

(IFOR'S Flat. CLARA, IFOR, with DAVID, chatting)

DAVID: Your Mam's right, Ifor. That blasted 'home by Xmas' talk…

CLARA: …same last year, and the years before, and all we got was bigger cemeteries. Makes my blood boil!

DAVID: And Zeppelins over our very heads. Do we stay on?

CLARA: No doubt of it!

DAVID: I've been through the accounts. We'll have to sell Cardiff. We can't run two salons.

IFOR: You've both got a base here for as long as you like.

DAVID: With your payments from teaching, Ifor, and your pennies from a song or two, my bit of pension, now I'm retiring, and Mam's tuition fees…

IFOR: … but the cost of that gypsy camp, Mam, lovely though it was, listen to that word, 'cost.'

CLARA: No! And look at us, the very picture of health. Tatler was right. Gave us a whole page, and the Dancing Ladies, headlines again. And your picture in the middle, Ifor, you looked so…romantic…

IFOR: Not you as well, Mam.

CLARA: Yes, me too, and don't you forget it!

DAVID: There's the war effort. All over the place that is.

CLARA: Even composers must fight for their country, and, when provoked, write patriotic songs for them. Right?

IFOR: Don't worry, I'm going to volunteer.

CLARA: I wouldn't go as far as that.

DAVID: You don't even know how to use a catapult.

IFOR: Listen, I have been saving and I am going to put down a deposit on a house not far from your gypsy wood. It has red roof tiles, so I'm calling it, 'Redroofs,' funny that. There'll be plenty of room there as well as here, Mam.

CLARA: Well, who'd have thought it? An accountant in the family. You've been marking up the takings, haven't you?! You're a good boy to your Mam. And your Dad, too. *(Kisses him)* Isn't he, Dad?

DAVID: Never better. And to dear Katie too.

IFOR: She's talking like mad now. So funny.

DAVID: So much better.

IFOR: All she needed was lots of hugs.

CLARA: Right! Now I've arranged a big concert for you at the old Alhambra, Ifor, with Sybil Vane, the best of my Ladies, with you as accompanist.

IFOR: Which song?

CLARA: Don't worry, not 'Song of Spring.'

IFOR: Which other one then?

CLARA: The one you're going to finish specially for it.

IFOR: Rejected by every management in town, and they still want me?

CLARA: Of course. 'Fools are always tardy.' Revelations.

DAVID: All due to your Mam, Ifor.

IFOR: To you both.

CLARA: Now that bloody war is raging, in spite of my peace efforts, you must write a patriotic song, like Tipperary.

IFOR: No one knows where Tipperary is.

CLARA: That doesn't matter, it's about our boys going to the front. Even I have written a little song for them, *(runs through voice exercises)* *(Sings)* 'Bring out your Flags, lads, think of all your Mams and all your Dads…'

IFOR: … that is dreadful…

CLARA: …bring out your…'

IFOR: …Mam, do shut up!

CLARA: It is patriotic.

IFOR: It is idiotic. Can't you see that?

CLARA: Then you write a better one…

IFOR:… I'm in the middle of half a dozen…

CLARA: …bet you can't do it.

IFOR: Bet I can.

CLARA: What do you think, Dafydd?

DAVID: I'm the great undeclared neutral, but I'm backing Ifor.

IFOR: There, you see!

CLARA *(To DAVID):* A traitor to your wife and helpmate, is it?!

IFOR: We all love you, Mam.

CLARA: You'd better! Well, the piano, get on with it. We're off to rehearsal. I'll tell your friends you're in the middle of a masterpiece again. That song, my son, must be ready for the Alhambra, by Friday!

IFOR: OK, OK! I got a whole lot on the boil, Mam.

CLARA: Well, I hope they've all been peeled! And you will be accompanist!

IFOR: Please, Mam, one success at a time.

CLARA: Get up and go, go!!

IFOR: Of course. I know!

(IFOR crosses over to piano, plays. CLARA and DAVID stand behind him, hands on his shoulders. CUT LIGHTS. EXIT CLARA, DAVD. Sound of piano continues, LIGHTS UP. IFOR scribbling on music sheets, discards them, starts again. Knock on door)

IFOR: Come in!

(ENTER KATIE with, duster, brush and pan)

KATIE: Mam said, excuse me, Ifor, would it be alright to do the room now?

IFOR: I don't see why not, Katie.

KATIE: I bought an old bucket and mop from the charity shop next door, so I'm ready for combat!

IFOR: Good news, Katie - *(He kisses her)* sister.

KATIE: Thank you, Ifor.

IFOR: Take the rest of the day off. Go on, go and look at the waters of the riding Thames, till I end my song. It's high tide about now, flows quiet and peaceful and smooth. Watch it go, flow with it and you'll be as calm and peaceful and that will wash away all your tears and fears...

KATIE: …there's lovely. Thank you. Ta. And do you want me to keep the fires burning while you're at home…

IFOR: … 'burning'? No ! …it's 'yearning!' That's it!

KATIE: Ta to you all, Ifor.

IFOR (*Scribbling madly*): Ta to you, too, Katie! The white storm is above and it is settling! Yes! 'Keep the Home Fires Burning…!'

(Scribbles feverishly. KATIE watching, adoring. FADE lights. Faint outline of fluttering white wings above IFOR. CUT LIGHTS. SOUND of wings flapping)

ACT 1 SCENE 8

(Side stage. BOBBY, EDDIE, watching through binoculars. Sound of plane wildly revving, swooping. EDDIE, BOBBY crouch, terrified)

BOBBY (*as commentator*): That, believe it or not, was Sub-lieutenant D Davies, of the Royal Naval Air Force, on his probationary flight here at the Crystal Palace Training Depot, now so far above us, but getting closer!

(Plane roars over them)

EDDIE: And all he said was he liked the uniform. I told Winnie, not the trenches, and he goes and puts him in the air! Even more dangerous.

BOBBY: And the uniform fitted like a glove.

EDDIE: He can't manage a sewing machine let alone a flying one.

BOBBY: They're signalling him to come in. Come on, Ifor. He's gone up again.

EDDIE: They're firing flares…

BOBBY: …at last, here he comes.

(Sound of plane stalling, firing, stalling, grinding crash. BOBBY, EDDIE Rush off. Sound of ambulance bells)

ACT 1 SCENE 9

(Spot side stage. IFOR wheeled on in wheel chair by EDDIE, BOBBY. Looks gorgeous in uniform; gets up, walks with cane, plaster up to the knee)

BOBBY: The War Office almost got rid of its top hero.

IFOR: I'm just an entertainer, I told them, not an aviator.

EDDIE: Well, I've fixed it. You're on a diplomatic mission as from now, even with the cane. To peaceful Sweden, a morale booster for the neutrals. A tour with songs and speeches. And then, concert parties in the trenches in France. All in uniform, of course, which you adore.

IFOR: Any Mam there with me?

BOBBY: Not this time.

IFOR: That must represent some sort of relief for the enemy.

(Gets out of chair, begins to walk with cane.)

IFOR *(Tapping good leg):* Don't worry, I've got another one.

(CROSS stage. EXIT)

ACT 1 SCENE 10

(LIGHTS UP front stage Flat area in shadow. Piano centre stage as on platform. Murmur of audience. IFOR side stage, nervous, in uniform. ENTER SYBIL. Audience applause. IFOR, begins playing. SYBIL sings, 'Keep the Home Fires Burning...' AUDIENCE joins in chorus. IFOR looking bemused, plays to end of song. Huge applause, cries of 'encore'! ENTER CLARA, DAVID, BOBBY, crowd round IFOR, embrace him. IFOR takes a bow, still limping. ALL return to Flat area. Lights up)

DAD: You've done it, son, you've done it!

BOBBY: Told you so! And did you hear, they joined in

IFOR: They seemed to know the chorus in advance.

CLARA: And next, Ifor, the grand Welsh opera.

IFOR: Mam, please, I am not a highbrow.

CLARA: Yes, you are!

IFOR: I am just a sort of…musical entertainer…

CLARA: …nonsense. A serious talent, just like me when I came home from America first time.

DAVID: Cheers to the whole lot of us, I say! Come on Clara, time for a bit of shopping.

CLARA: And I'm keeping a keen eye on that leg. No steeple chasing, alright?

(Blows kiss. DAVID, CLARA EXIT)

BOBBY: Encore! Encore!

IFOR: What do you think of the Paris cabaret show I gave you?

BOBBY: Your ' dirty rat!' outline? Most exotic thing I've ever read.

IFOR: Not too wild?

BOBBY: It'll stun them. But ease off a bit, Ifor. You've just had terrific song successes, all in the bag, published, so take a day off, then we can talk about this amazing entertainment known, elegantly, as 'The Rat.' I loved that!

IFOR: Good title eh? By the way don't mention it to Mam. She wants me embalmed in some sort of opera at Covent Garden.

BOBBY: Don't worry, Ifor, we'll escape together.

IFOR: Got 'The Rat' cast. Here. See what you think. Acting copies.

BOBBY: You have been a busy little bee, Ifor.

IFOR: You've got the second male lead and Eddie's put in his own cash again too.

BOBBY: Bless our Eddie, and his hundred talents! I'll send these out now. Just sit still then for five minutes. No more plane stunts! OK? Play, song, show, film, - play, song, show, film - the monstrously tasty Novello work-sandwich!

IFOR: You and your sandwiches! I can't help it, Bobby, it's the Mam spell, got to get down to it. And it's lucky that both of us love what we're doing.

(CUT LIGHTS, SOUND)

ACT 1 SCENE 11

(Sound of lapping water, evening, traffic. SPOT ON CLARA, KATIE talk by Thames)

KATIE: 'Try to enjoy everything,' Ifor said.

CLARA *(Sings)*: 'Where is my wondering boy tonight'?! *(They laugh)* What you been up to, to get so much better?

KATIE: Just walking, talking, like now. The removal people seemed a good crowd over the new piano. So cheerful. Then a walk. Covent Garden. I watched a potter at his trade in the market, then went on to the picture house and enjoyed my little stay there. Travel is nice. I bet visiting Katmandu would be fun! Your Ifor is right. I look at the waters here every day, and then I feel calm, like the waves. The blows and the buffets are fading. Sorry about my expressions, my English is somewhat disjointed today. Why's Ifor have everything in white?

CLARA: ' Wondrous are thy dwellings, O Lord!'

KATIE: Funny havin' to think in English.

CLARA: You'll get used to it. But I had to read the whole of the Old Testament out loud to get the accent right. Duw, English is so good for voice training.

KATIE: Ifor don't have no trouble with English, do he?

CLARA: With his memory? Never. Music he learned it all he did when he was curled up in there *(pats stomach),* just like a normal baby, except for his conk! Half his singing he got in the womb. *(Runs through voice scale)* I saw to that.

KATIE: Fancy, Mam, miraclus.

CLARA: Quite. He got prizes in Oxford for language. Everybody should be bi-lingual, you are getting like that, and Ifor is tri-lingual.

KATIE: Why's everybody down here is dying of this 'thrombosis.' Only my Dad did that at home, but he fell off a garden wall first. Then the funeral. Mostly old people, one teenager. Me. I behaved well, and looked nice too, I think. And Ifor over his leg already. Marvlus. Duw there's lovely, the waters tonight.

CLARA: You're sounding fine now.

KATIE: Except for my attack of hiccoughs last week, lovely, but just an echo now. Mam, could I ask, I do early sales so I don't buy clothes at in Xmas, well this morning, I saw, noticed, a very nice deep purple three-quarter length jacket in te charity shop, it only needs some sewing in the seams and shortening of the arm, and hey presto, ready for Winter. Only, hope you don't mind my mentioning, two pounds…

CLARA: …let's go and buy it right now!

KATIE: You're all so lovely here, my Mam is always sayin' that too, and all your Ladies! I'll soon be right to go home, I think.

CLARA: Of course.

KATIE: And the greengrocer outside, he gave me two good looking cabbages, this morning, for free!

CLARA: You Katie are a credit to the best mother and father and brother and the best choir in Great Britain! Now, to the jacket! And home quick then.

KATIE: More and more thanks it is, Mam.

CLARA: Another first night. You can help me dress. Seats in the Royal Box. I wave to the audience, like that and like that…

KATIE *(Waving):* …like that.

CLARA: And they wave back to me! And don't forget Ifor's rice pudding for the morning.

(They laugh. Walk off, waving. EXIT)

ACT 1 SCENE 12

(MONTHS later. Late night. IFOR'S Flat. BOBBY, DAVID pacing, listening. Sounds of distant applause, bangings from theatre downstairs. BOBBY looks out of window. Street noises, traffic, pigeons)

DAVID: Was that a cheer again? And that?

BOBBY: Sounds like a breakers' yard.

DAVID: Mam was all against this 'French decadence,' as she called it but…

BOBBY: …she was all for 'success' too.

DAVID: …in a cellar bar and cabaret, in notorious Monmartre…

BOBBY: …shocking!

DAVID: …full of villains and…harlots. After all Ifor's triumphs, she couldn't sit through 'such a low show.' And that bar…?

BOBBY: …'The White Coffin.'

DAVID: Not cheery at all. I mean the entrance doors were coffin-shaped, the ash trays and fittings too. Morbid. Of course it looked good, all white and glossy, but when I saw those tarts, I nearly left in embarrassment, Mam too. Mam said…'my beautiful, son, playing a rat in a brothel house!' And that 'Apache dance,' they were downright near touching each others' privates. The peg-top trousers, suited Ifor, but that long grey muffler, he should have used it to cover up himself more. And I thought 'apache' was Geronimo, not that gang of Parisian evil-doers and low-lifes.

BOBBY *(Imitating CLARA)*: '…you can't say that, Ifor!' 'But Mother stayed too! *(Looks out of window)* Audience still crowding outside stage door.

DAVID: And didn't that Noel warn Ifor that French apaches were not for London audiences.

BOBBY: You don't listen to that Coward twerp, do you?
DAVID: No, I don't.

BOBBY: Ifor's parties are little republics for friends from all walks of life, not a court for snobs and blue-bloods, like Noel's.

DAVID: Why are we waiting for so long? *(Listens)* That funny banging sound.

BOBBY: What is the people's verdict then?

DAVID: Whatever, I'll love him just the same.

(ENTER EDDIE, laughing, carrying newspapers. Sudden burst of cheers)

BOBBY: What is up down there, Eddie?

EDDIE: Mam's putting on a great show tonight!

(Spot on side stage. CLARA standing in 'box' waving graciously to audience, curtseying and blowing kisses. More cheers. KATIE hides behind CLARA, in her 'three-quarter' purple jacket. IFOR enters, sees MAM, covers his eyes and rushes off. Audience cheer every time CLARA waves)

EDDIE: We had to lock them out back stage.

BOBBY: What was that thumping sound?

EDDIE: Stamping for encores. Nineteen in all. After each encore, pounding feet more, more of that Apache dance. And Ifor gave it to them. Went mad. Magnificent. Tried to climb onto stage. Ifor had to run for it. They would have clawed the shirt off his back. Had to lock them out. Fans out in the Strand now. Look.

(ENTER CLARA, breathless, with newspaper, ENTER KATIE with early reviews. Hands them out)

CLARA: One of my best performances, I think!

(ALL read. Noises below)

CLARA: I can't believe it, still hammering away, although I did help to keep them calm.

KATIE: I thought we was lost although Ifor had won!

(CLARA motions to KATIE. KATIE EXITS)

BOBBY *(Reading out)*: 'Terrific fun! All the audience had to do was sit back and enjoy it!'

DAVID: 'Another triumph.'

EDDIE *(Looking from window):* And they're still waiting in the street.

BOBBY: Needed a battering ram to push them all in, and a vacuum cleaner to suck them all out!

EDDIE: It'll take about £1,500 a week, I'd say. And it's definite for film rights, too, no doubt of it.

(RE-ENTER KATIE with bundle of printed sheet music, and posters of the 'rat' dance. Holds one up)

KATIE: Back stage selling like hot scones, in the foyer too, even people doing the rat dance in the street!

BOBBY *(Of posters)*: Where did you get these, Katie?

EDDIE: I took this little opportunity, just in case. Sheet music for 'the Dance of the Apache, with the steps, a foxtrot, by its creator, Ivor the Magnificent Novello on the cover! See!

CLARA: Well, you sly boots.

(Sound of running steps on stairs. IFOR erupts in, in 'Apache' costume. He bows. Kisses MAM, IFOR and CLARA do a parody apache dance! ALL cheer. Spot on NEWSVENDOR, side stage)

NEWSVENDOR (*In broad cockney*): Star, News, Stannard! Read all about it! *(Looks over 'crowds')* Blimey, haven't they got a home to go to? Read all about it. 'The Rat' wows West End.' That's what I calls 'news. Triumph of Novello. I should think so, been hummin' his songs since I was a nipper. God bless you up there, for giving us, Ifor The Rat! And bugger all 'hostilities!' *(Loud cheers)* Read all about it!

(CUT LIGHTS, SOUND)

ACT 1 SCENE 13

(Morning. Six months later. The Flat. BOBBY at table going through contracts, with EDDIE. EDDIE tries a few slides with projector onto screen. The Choir Ladies, scenes from plays, playbills, Hollywood stars. ENTER KATIE)

KATIE: Mam said it was alright to say good bye for now to you all and say I thank yous like mad. Never forget it. My Mam, contralto she is, she's ill, but you all know that, but I'll be visiting here. Mam said so and Ifor too when I wishes. Imagine. Thank you.

EDDIE: Goodbye, Katie. Have lots of luck.

KATIE: You too.

BOBBY: Bye, Katie. Keep going.

KATIE: I will, I will. There's lovely you are.

(KATIE embraces each one. EXITS)

BOBBY: She's over that nasty bit of experience of hers, called 'life.'

EDDIE: See what friends can do.

(ENTER IFOR)

EDDIE: Thank God. *(Puts on slides)* Look, Ifor, Your friends all over the shop, Ronald Coleman, Gary Grant, Errol Flynn…

BOBBY: Naughty boys, those two!

EDDIE: …Hitchcock, Joan Crawford, 'Me Tarzan' Johnny Weismuller, Vivien Lee, Marlene Dietrich…

IFOR: …and naughty girls those two as well.

EDDIE: Your special fans! All there. All former Redroofs inmates, with you at the top step!

IFOR: Great people, great times. Those faces went past too quickly. All I wanted to say, was, stay awhile longer friends. Stop! And no more goodbyes. Our Katie, she said goodbye? Bless her.

EDDIE: *(Of slides)* …you see all these?! Proof positive. You are now an established theatre composer, Ifor, for good! And actor, and face! That profile! as matinee idol, you heard the women. And, by the way, the film rights of 'The Rat' sold. You are my top prize, ifor, all my love for poems and plays and songs, and boys of promise! Thank you, my own dearest Ifor!

IFOR: Lovely, Eddie, one of the few sensible people with money I know! You turn gold into talent! But, there is so much to learn. I am a mere novice.

EDDIE: Excellent.

IFOR: That's my Dad.

EDDIE: 'Get up and go!'

IFOR: We all know who that is!

BOBBY: Nose to the grindstone.

EDDIE: That's how he got that profile. Bobby, help me. Look, Ifor, apart from 'We'll keep the Home Fires…' look at the playbills here, you have worked with the best - Ben Travers, PG Wodehouse, Jerome Kern, and the loveliest stars, Gladys Cooper, Constance Cummings, apart from the apaches, who all adore you, you now have a totally romantic public image…

IFOR: …I'm just a failed choir boy, basically, a rejected song writer, childless, without issue, as they say. But look to my Mam and my Dad, that's where I'm really blessed. My music, films, shows were all so much a matter of luck.

EDDIE: No, they were not - a gift of the Gods.

IFOR: …the chalk-white notations of my imagination?

BOBBY: …that's the gift, Ifor.

EDDIE: Listen to the music in the titles alone, 'The Radiance of your Eyes,' 'The Golden Moth,' 'Our Nell' for the Empire Year! Eleven numbers in Act 1 alone. And 'Arlette,' from the French, by you, your hit, the whole show… not to forget the unforgettable 'The Rat.' Memorable, on the dance floors of England to this very day!

BOBBY: From the Prince of Pomania, to the Count of Luxembourg, to the Druid Singers of Camelot, to the dirty French rat! Even Mam could not stop any of that.

EDDIE: Just keep it up, Ifor, I beg.

IFOR: So much fun. 'Gifts' mean giving…'

BOBBY: …your old granddad that was…

IFOR: And my, 'Land of Might Have Been,' with lyrics by… who?

BOBBIE, **IFOR:** Edward Marsh!

(They applaud. Toast EDDIE. EDDIE takes a bow)

EDDIE: Your publishers are going mad with all the music of money!

IFOR: Well, here are the updated contracts. What do you think?

BOBBY: Let's have a look.

EDDIE: You still serious about joining up, Ifor?

IFOR: Why not?

EDDIE: You've seen the casuality lists? Enough to kill all the standing civilians in the land, and not with bullets, just grief will do, grief does the rounds every day, like the milkman, I've seen him.

IFOR: Me, too.

EDDIE: Back to business, my boys.

BOBBY: A pleasure.

IFOR: Hope you don't mind, Eddie, but, you've invested in most of my shows…

EDDIE: ….and never lost a penny.

BOBBY: Where do you raise the money, Ifor is asking?

EDDIE: I don't mind you asking, Ifor, curiosity always becomes the gifted. I had a huge inheritance. Far too big for decency. So I decided to invest it in all the talents of the gifted young that I met, personally, or through my Agency. Alright, you say, but where do the coffers come from? I'll tell you. From my great, great, great, Grandfather, Spencer Percival, Prime Minister of England in 1809, and the only PM ever to be assassinated, on this occasion by a lunatic banker in 1912 in the lobby of the House of Commons. Well, my granddad was very popular, and he left twelve children, a grieving wife, and a shocking memory for England, so the Cabinet, shook up, and generous to a fault, for once, voted his widow an income of 50,000 a year to be left in perpetuity. I inherited the lot, my murder money, I call it, and I use it to create those who really bear the gift of life, especially the young boys disappearing in Picardy, thw Somme, the Dardanelles, all over the globe. I didn't want to see an ounce of real talent wasted or forgotten. Bless Rupert, at least I recognised his genius and his beauty, boys, too, almost in time. And dear, 'mad' Sassoon. My Georgian Collections of Drinkwater, Masefield, Graves, Flecker, all rescued from the grave. See, Ifor, that's where the money comes from, 'murder,' Ifor, and that's where does it go to, life - with my blessings. So any lad you feel is gifted, let me know.

And you two here, you are my young champions, the gatherers and deliverers of all that's best in this all too brief glimpse of life. Now, Ifor, how did you get on in the dragon's den of that publisher?

IFOR: I managed to get twenty-five a year as a retainer. What do you think, Eddie?

EDDIE: That's good. Stay with it.

BOBBY: Brilliant, even with the big hits.

EDDIE: Your powers of persuasion are magical, my Ifor!

BOBBY: And his beauty even more so, Eddie.

IFOR: Down, boys, down. Now, what about a three-penny royalty on each copy of sheet music? Did I do OK?

EDDIE: That is astonishing. But you're a dreamer, you can name your price!

BOBBY: I think I second that thought, although I'm not sure I know quite what it means!

EDDIE: Notorious liars, publishers, might back out any time. Miserly to a 't'.' Accept by return, Ifor.

IFOR: They've also agreed to spend five-hundred on extra publicity.

BOBBY: Don't need that, Eddie. Your songs are their own publicity. And 'Home Fires' is still everywhere, music halls, Palm Courts, tea lounges, family parlours phonographs, the front line trenches - on all sides! Where next?

IFOR: To your next male lead…

BOBBY: …a mandarin with his moustaches. Love it!

EDDIE: Listen, I had this from Winnie himself, even the French troops have taken up 'Home Fires,' some of them thought it was the British National anthem! And more popular with the Yanks now than 'Tipperary!'

(ENTER CLARA, in a rush)

CLARA: Hear that! Listen! Listen! *(SOUND of 'Home Fires' being played on barrel organ outside)* On a barrel organ, never would have thought it, for the people, see, everybody who passes by. Paid him a pound to keep handle going all day outside the theatre! But what I say is 'Keep the Peace Fires Burning!' I am against this bloody war, and with your dear friend Rupert, killed in action!

EDDIE: 'He turned naturally towards the light, like a flower.'

CLARA: Of course he did. Eddie, I am so sorry. And it is the same all over the whole land. Everyone now knows the grief that comes of lost sons and daughters, it lasts generations.

EDDIE: Bravo, Clara! I'm with you. The war to end all wars!

BOBBY: But I feel the war-mongers are going to be hard to beat. First the war effort, and now the peace one. Don't know which is worse.

CLARA: We ladies, we've made a start, Bobby. I've just come directly from our first meeting, 'The Women's League for Peace' is now officially inaugurated. We have established a General Council, and our Chairlady is the Countess of Oxford, no less, with myself, and Dame Sybil Thorndike on our platform, to name but a few. We've organised a mass rally at the Albert Hall, with my new anthem, 'Keep the Peace Fires Going' I say, conducted by myself and my Royal Ladies' Choir of Wales! No more wars!

IFOR: Ah, Mam, you look so lovely in full sail!

BOBBY: Bless her and all who sail in her!

EDDIE: On with the song!

(Spot side stage, BARREL ORGANIST plays 'HOME FIRES')

EDDIE: And royalties, I've been meaning to mention it, Ifor, she gobbles them up,

IFOR: Can't say no to my Mam.

EDDIE: Why not?

IFOR: She's my Mam, my white goddess!

EDDIE: I don't doubt it! But these concerts and travels, sometimes she claims even when they've never happened.

IFOR: I salute her imagination!

EDDIE: Eight trunks on tour just for herself. Block bookings for friends of the Choir. Beauty Parlours, bills in five languages. And this one, fifty pounds, for a purple Roman toga, with gold Grecian sandals.

IFOR: She looked stunning in those.

EDDIE: But your royalties fritter away.

IFOR: She is a touch extravagant, I agree. But the expense is for others, for her choir, her concerts. I'll have to write more hits, Eddie, don't worry. And don't forget to transfer funds into Dad's accounts now he's taking retirement.

EDDIE: As you say, Ifor.

IFOR: One hit, however global, is simply is not enough for a family like mine! What's the time? Thought film directors were supposed to be punctual.

BOBBY: He'll be here.

IFOR: Does our French film genius, Monsieur Louis Mercanton, know the way?

BOBBY: Got a good track record, speaks English, of a sort.

IFOR: And I French, wonderfully. Is it really true Eddie? He was just looking through piles of photos of actors in your office, on the off chance, saw my photo on the wall… go on…

EDDIE: '…that's the man I want for lead.' It's true. Fairly shouted at me, 'Forget the others.' 'But our Ifor is a composer,' I said, humouring the lunatic.' 'Then lead me to him!' he ordered. That really is as it was. Your Mam was not pleased when she heard you were going on stage, in a film, 'just as bad,' she said. She wants that Welsh grand opera, Ifor.

IFOR: Bless her. I'm happy she's on tour. That's her genius. Well, the film tycoon is late.

BOBBY: Not yet, Ifor, still got a minute. *(Bell rings)* There, see, he's even early - by fifty-five seconds!

(EXIT BOBBY, RE-ENTERS leading MR MERCANTON. MERCANTON stares fixedly at IFOR, circles him, looking at him from different angles. EDDIE switches on slides, shows IFOR doing Apache dance. MERCANTON transfixed by IFOR and the dance)

MERCANTON: Magnifique! Est-ce-que tu danses aussi?

IFOR: Pas avec une jambe cassée.

MERCANTON: Mon hero.

IFOR: 'Comedien' s'il te plait.

BOBBY: En anglais s'il te plait!

(MERCANTON'S outlines plot with wild gestures)

MERCANTON: Ifor, film is 'The Call of Blood,' of adultery, revenge, mon ami. They are in hot Sicily on honeymoon, Maurice the man, you do that, but wife is called away, so you has passion with local girl, two big erreurs, the father find out and murder Maurice. Wife returns, finds Maurice dead on rocks. But put flowers on graves, in tears. It is fate. All is forgiveness.

EDDIE *(Aside)*: What you think, Bobby?

BOBBY: Good as any tosh Ifor could invent.

EDDIE: Bobby! Sounded a bit like Noel there.

BOBBY: Noel's just jealous. Ifor is not. Ifor's imagination is firmly based in Ruritania, Noel's in the Imperial War Museum. Take your pick.

MERCANTON: Here, my slides for location. Hold it still. Perfect. We will be on location in Taormina, hot sun, handsome tan. I see, yes, first night premiere, Ivor Novello, new international screen star! You get many offers, but you take mine first.

IFOR: 'On location,' you said.

MERCANTON: During all takes, yes. Village all ready for us, even now I have arranged fiesta for whole population. Turn head to side. Perfect. Now, you bad husband. Creep into bedroom of local girl when your wife away nursing sick Papa. Ok. Now leap on her. Seduce. Very good. Now do dead on mountain side. Her father has killed you dead for honour of family. No, do angoisse! She see you dead, she kill herself. Never mind moaning, groaning, this silent film. OK, not theatre. Then next, you try Miarka, child of the Bear…

IFOR: …pardon.

MERCANTON: Next film. Ready too. This about Miarka, foster mother was performing bear. No, don't do bear. Go to zoo first. Miarka betrothed. Do that, like give ring. OK. Ivor, you play Ivor on old donkey with Desdemona, the blood calls, no that first film, then she discover you, Ivor, are real lover, dies giving thanks to Saint Peter in church. Gypsy funeral. All burn! Do. Do! *(IFOR does various poses)* That good, all good, you look good, Ivor. Good when without word, and you got good voice. You get all ladies flapping when they see. Agreable, Ifor?

IFOR: Yes, very agreeable, monsieur! Eddie, I have need of you again.

EDDIE: Now, the contracts, Monsieur Mercanton…

BOBBY: …and a few parts for me too.

MERCANTON: That is good and done, mon ami!
(FADE SOUND, LIGHTS)

ACT 2 SCENE 1

(Ten years later. IFOR'S flat. Sunshine. BOBBY, EDDIE now much older, going through papers, contracts. Cuttings. EDDIE operates slide machine with photos of IFOR, for press and publicity. Box of gifts for IFOR)

EDDIE: Not all so long ago, Bobby.

BOBBY: And the Kaiser fled to Tulip Land. And his army to the beer halls of the Reich.

But now they've got this guttersnipe Kaiser, one Herr Hitler.

EDDIE: End of story.

BOBBY: Or the beginning.

EDDIE: Never.

BOBBY: Humans adore human wastage. A fact.

EDDIE: Well, I'm not going to stop trying.

BOBBY: Like our Clara. But the Armistice was no winner.

EDDIE: Better than nothing.

BOBBY: All the talent in those twenty-mile long graveyards?

EDDIE: Don't…

BOBBY: …sorry, Eddie. There, there, you've saved lots, you really have.

EDDIE: You, Ifor, yes…so our little Katie's back for a visit?

BOBBY: She comes and goes. Open house really. Her Mam's sick too. Ifor sent down the best doctor here.

BOBBY: Good for Ifor. And this, the usual box of fan gifts, what did we get today? Six neckties, scarves by the dozen, a pressure cooker, leather-bound version of Tennyson. Keep that, he likes Tennyson. Let's have a look – lobelias, hollyhocks, lilies, begonias, yew branches, in gold flake. Yes. All to the hospitals again. I'll take them downstairs.

EDDIE: Don't know where Ifor gets the energy. We should do another of Bobby's 'sandwiches', to remind him how hard he's working. Got to take a break. And I don't mean tours of the Med, or Jamaica, or the States again, I mean, rest!

BOBBY *(Looking at photos):* Trouble is Ifor looks good in any costume. They'd print any of these.

EDDIE: We'll just have to choose the best ones.

BOBBY: After you, Edde. You'll be here all week.

EDDIE: All of them are the best.

(IFOR leaps onto stage, dressed in cloak, hat of 18th century Venice)

BOBBY: My God, the Venetian gallant, Count Vittoria!

IFOR: Note the tricorn hat, the velvet cloak, the sword, the shoulder length wigs, full of fleas, I have fallen in lust with Leonora, wife of voluptuary aristocrat, Almoro who crushes my hands in a wine press so I can't fence, but my love poisons Almoro, then I finish him off in a duel by the skin of my teeth, just before greeting the two angelic dwarves at Court, but I get a sort of cummupence, here's me flat on my back on the quay of a canal, my head in the water. Exit the Venetian Welshman. The interiors were shot in Berlin of all places.

BOBBY: …and your film career is over the top!

EDDIE *(Projects slides):* What about your 'Carnival' film here?

IFOR: Bad about the film, lovely about me. There, that one's 'The Bohemian Girl,' a Princess of Gypsies, why so many gypsies in my life? But in fact I'm not, I'm a polish Count Thaddeus here, in hiding from the Austrian invaders. Hit song 'I Dreamt I Dwelt in Marble Halls' and got married to lovely Gladys. Oh, I forgot, I was put to sleep for two hundred years in between but was brought back for the love of a good woman…I forget the rest. What film was it next I moved to, Eddie?

EDDIE: 'A Man without Desire?'

IFOR: No, that was the previous one.

EDDIE: We've got to get all your work in order, Ifor, for the royalties.

IFOR: I'm doing my best.

EDDIE: We must sandwich them all together again. What next?

BOBBY: The great DW Griffith! Another Taff! Not a happy day.

EDDIE: 'The White Rose,' an acknowledged flop.

IFOR: One of my best.

EDDIE: What?

IFOR: I learned a thing or two.

BOBBY: And the American papers voted you 'the handsomest man in England.'

IFOR: Tosh. Never more embarrassed in my life. Move on.

BOBBY: They voted in droves for you. Ramon Navarro, Valentino pushed to last place.

IFOR: Rot, Bobby. Stop there.

EDDIE: Here's you, a prim curate, in 'A Man of Sin!'

IFOR: And you Eddie did splendidly, sued our Griffith for 11,000 dollars, sixteen weeks of salary, and won. Ta, Eddie.

BOBBY *(Slide of IFOR as BONNIE PRINCE CHARLIE)*: Bonnie Prince Charlie!

IFOR: I loved those tartan skirts.

BOBBY: And Flora MacDonald often took them off.

EDDIE: There you lie, dead before a very large Protestant candle at the high altar. And now to the immense 'Rat.' Never seen so many photos.

IFOR: Well, a Parisian apache was a change from a Romany rogue. And there's the nightclub, everything coffin shaped, my devisement, even the doorways, underworld thugs and floozies galore. And I loved my famous dance. Like that and that!

BOBBY: King Rat, 'you are now one of the world's supreme young men of the screen,' it says here. You rotten old matinee idol!

IFOR: I told you, Bobby, knock off that rot, svp!

BOBBY: Just what it says here.

IFOR: Concentrate on the royalties.

BOBBY: Done!

EDDIE: Here's the final figures.

IFOR: Good stuff! I can now afford my mother. And her Ladies.

EDDIE: They're going a bit gray too. And some have even gone home to their grandkids.

IFOR: Grey? Aren't we all? *(Holds up photo)* Look, me with a muffler, a real ghoul, I reveal myself in very grisly circumstances - as the Limehouse Ripper! Take that, and that! Bloody good bits and that new Director, Hitchcock, was really on the ball. And then 'Downhill,' that was me, not good. Hitchcock to the rescue.

BOBBY: That was 'The Vortex,' bloody Noel Coward's play, not a friend of yours Ifor.

IFOR: Nothing wrong with dear Noel, just spits a bit too much, that's all.

BOBBY: …and in public.

IFOR: 'The Constant Nymph!' I paid off Redroofs with the fee from that. Heart and soul of a thousand parties!! Thanks again, Eddie.

BOBBY: And now, a charming love story set in an Austro-Hungarian military barracks!" I give you, 'The Gallant Hussar!'

IFOR: And you can take him back, that film had such little plot I always thought I was making my first entrance.

EDDIE: Look at the receipts, Ifor.

IFOR: A terrific film!

BOBBY: 'The Return of the Rat?'

IFOR: Against my better judgement.

EDDIE: A 'South Sea Bubble…'

BOBBY: An indisputable flop. You in a yachting cap, that public school sweater, that pipe, and my god, that moustache!

IFOR: Not entirely my favourite photo I must say.

EDDIE: And now the great divide, 'Symphony in Two Flats,' the talkies are here, and your first voice film which was 'melodious, like a nightingale…very, very pleasant with its Welsh lilt…'

IFOR: …do not read it out, Bobby, especially when the birds are singing. OK?

BOBBY: Well, your voice works, Ifor.

IFOR: Lots lost out on that. Grateful I am, I swear!

EDDIE: Then your re-make of 'The Lodger.'

IFOR: A bloody downright disaster. 'Once a Lady,' 'I Lived with You,' and 'Autumn Crocus'… all flops I fell right through them right back onto the stage! The stage is a paradise but also one of the most cruel and treacherous places in the world. So watch your cash, Bobby, like our Eddie here. He's a genius at that, bless you.

EDDIE: Nobody except you Ifor ever had the courage to throw his whole heart at the feet of an audience…

BOBBY: …and seen them always pick it up. Marvellous.

IFOR: Ah, friendship is all. One day, I want it – as composer, writer, deviser, all the receipts, the last of the original actor/managers, in total charge. Every bird, note of music, beat of heart, glowing accounts, all my own work, like the pavement artists of old! Mine. Mine! I do not say that my plays are better than anyone else's, but they are apparently right for me. Whenever I have been in a play of mine, it has never failed. In somebody else's play, the flops come Nothing but the truth for my fans out there, the truth of the imagination. I have so many ideas, teeming in my poor brain. I must get up and go, go, go! I'll do it yet. Silver screens, here I come again.

BOBBY: Well, It was films that made you an actor, Ifor. I said to Mercanton, if you can teach Ifor to act, you can teach stones to dance.

IFOR: You are a true mate, Bobby!

EDDIE *(Packs up slides, ready to go)*: I tell you what, apart from the moustache photo, I'll just have copies made, and send out the lot. Then it's their problem. Prepare yourself for the film moguls, Ifor.

(Kisses IFOR, BOBBY. EDDIE EXITS)

IFOR: Time's right I think. Mam's away setting up another artists' colony in Pembrokeshire, Dad's visiting old friends in Cardiff. He's getting on a bit. Still, Katie's good company for him. You know Bobby, I've never been able to get up in the morning without a feeling of my impending doom. Ever get that?

BOBBY: Yes, except weekends.

IFOR: When that day comes, what I'd like, is to die making an enchanting curtain speech after a successful first night to the sound of cheers, then drop down peacefully dead before the curtain falls.

BOBBY: Anything to escape.

IFOR: No one escapes. That's the bloody rub! So carpe diem, enjoy the day. *(Looking into mirror)* Enough wrinkles to sink a battleship. Hair's intact though. No dewlaps. Another gift, Master Time, my thanks. Look at that airy-fairy mug in the glass, Bobby.

BOBBY: Good enough for me.

IFOR: *(Looking in mirror):* I love you better with a tan, Ifor.

BOBBY: You sure you want to tackle California again?

IFOR: I adore all sunshine. See Mam's old friends, flatter a few directors, watch them fall for me again, the handsome fools. For fun!

BOBBY: But under contract to the Studio, you've got no freedom.

IFOR: Oh, yes I have. And the redoubtable Eddie is behind me. And I'm so pretty.

BOBBY: Sorry, I was a bit way out about it.

(IFOR disrobes, down to his pants)

IFOR: You were right, my Bobby, keeps my feet firmly planted to the ground. 'The handsomest man in England.' Look at me. My feet, to begin with. They're much too big for my spindly old legs, see. And look at my bony old chest, undeveloped, hardly any muscle, see the ribs, made like that, not through dieting, and my arms, look, like a beggars, emaciated. My neck like a column, thank God for good news at last. And then the whole rests on the profile, my conk, which just happened to fit. And the hair, see the strands of gray. See the little crow's feet. Look at my neck, like a turkey's one day, the circles of wrinkles, ending there and there. Look at me, Bobby, you see what I mean, apart from the top bit, I am most decidedly NOT the handsomest man in England. And I am Welsh anyway. And now I think I'll take in some of the sunshine out there. Come on, dear Bobby, join me on the sun terrace. And I'm serious about playing Henry V one day!

(BOBBY, IFOR arm in arm, EXIT to terrace. Faint sounds of fluttering wings. CUT LIGHTS, SOUND)

ACT 2 SCENE 2

(Film studio, in darkness. *Sound of animal snuffling, gruniing. Fade. Dim light. In shadow, IFOR in TARZAN costume. GRETA GARBO, TALLULAH BANKHEAD, in JANE costume, make up to TARZAN)*

IFOR: Unhand me, Jane. Me Tarzan!

GRETA: Me not Jane. Me Greta Garbo. You are lovely, Ifor.

TALLULAH: Me not Jane either. Me Tallulah Bankhead. You are beautiful, Ifor.

GRETA: Come, Tarzan, we go to myhigh party now.

TALLULAH: Come, Tarzan, we go to my thigh party now.

(ENTER GORILLA, beating chest. GRETA, TALLULAH TARZAN RUN OFF IN TERROR. EXIT IFOR pursued by GORILLA)

ACT 2 SCENE 3

(IFOR'S Flat. Five years later. Morning. EDDIE pacing with BOBBY)

BOBBY: I told you, the bombers would get through.

EDDIE: Madness. After twenty years, more of the same. I won't give in, Bobby

BOBBY: They'll close us all down.

EDDIE: Life has to go on.

BOBBY: On stage and off. At least the shows keep surviving.

EDDIE: Why does Tennent want to see Ifor?

BOBBY: Ifor is/was a Holywood star I suppose.

EDDIE: 'A Hollywood flop,' Ifor describes it. 'A waste of time.' 'Me Tarzan!' I mean! No, I think it's because Harry Tennant needs a success. Drury Lane has a capacity of over 2,500, and it's failing fast, playing to barley twenty per cent. Disasterous.

BOBBY: Does our Ifor know, the appointment ?

EDDIE: No, Binkie just rang.

BOBBY: That Binkie went up faster than a rocket. Old partner of Ifor's, I believe.

EDDIE: They're still friends.

BOBBY: Ifor's tanned and gorgeous, so watch out!

EDDIE: And here he is.

(ENTER IFOR, agitated. Kisses them both)

EDDIE: Ifor…

IFOR: …Mam welcomes me back with the usual balls ups, so to speak. Only stayed a couple of weeks in her new 'colony,' and now they're after me for the bills. Here. Take care of them, will you, Eddie.

EDDIE: The bills come to over £12,000, Ifor.

IFOR: Stage manager's ill again, cigars and chocolates to the hospital. *(Of box of presents)* Take some of those

BOBBY: Leave it to me.

IFOR: Hire a special train for the next Redroofs bash. And cars for the guests who're inconvenienced.

EDDIE: More films in the air, Ifor?

IFOR: Films! In the can, and that's that. On stage, you learn something new every night. One day, I swear I will play Henry V. I will! Might even keep Mam quiet! Now the real news. They've named an ice cream after me, 'Bombe Ivor Novello,' at the Caprice.

EDDIE: True success!

IFOR: What's the non news?

EDDIE: Harry M Tennent himself wants you to have lunch with him.

IFOR: Really? Why?

EDDIE: He never says 'why.' But he did say 'when.'

IFOR: When?

EDDIE: In an hour, at the Caprice. Have you got anything in your files which might pass as a show?

IFOR: No, been too busy getting a tan.

BOBBY: Binkie put in a word for you.

IFOR: Excellent!

EDDIE: Good luck.

IFOR: Thank God for your happy, happy faces!

(EXIT IFOR in a rush)

ACT 2 SCENE 4

(Murmur of diners, cutlery, bottles clinking. Spot on table. HARRY TENNENT and IFOR, end of meal, sipping coffee)

IFOR: Well, you've got enough other shows to keep you going. I mean you run half the West End.

HARRY: But Drury Lane has the potential for magnificent profits. All we get is loss after loss with every show we put on. We need another 'Cavalcade…'

IFOR: …Noel's most patriotic success. Good for him.

HARRY: He's tied up with film offers at the moment.

IFOR: I've just come back from the States. And what do I find here, more American musicals than in New York. Why don't you try native composers and writers for a change.

HARRY: Heard you'd gone a bit 'native?' yourself. Tarzan, the Ape Man. 'Me Tarzan, you Jane.' Did you really write that?

IVOR: You don't write words like that, Harry, you grunt them.

HM: Well, it's a huge success. Something 'new,' you said.

IFOR: Pardon?

HM: I know you cunning Welsh lot by now, Binkie warned me. He sends his best. You were friends once, right?

IFOR: And still friends – friendly friends. OK.

HARRY: You've got something up your sleeve, haven't you?

IFOR: What?! Me? Never.

HARRY: You came because you've got something in mind, haven't you? Come on.

IVOR (*pretending to search for words*): Well, now you mention it….

HARRY: … I knew it! Out with it!

IVOR: I've hardly got anything…

HARRY: …then make it up…go on!

IFOR: …you mean, **now**?

HARRY: You've got five minutes.

IFOR: Flash!

HARRY: What?

IFOR: Flash! Yes. Flash!

HARRY: What are you saying, Ifor?

IFOR: The whole show just flashed before my eyes, in white heat!

HARRY: You sure?

IFOR: Listen, spontaneous combustion! Broadly, a mix of royal romance, gypsy wedding, murder, sinking liners, shipwrecks, opera belladonnas, an Empress, a palace ballroom, a cast of thousands. Plot! King Stefan of Krasnia loves Militza, a gypsy prima donna, whom he has heard at a gala performance, ending in an attempt on her life. The hero appears, the inventor of this new TV thing. Moving pictures you know, everyone will be amazed. Romance married to the new technology. The lovers run away, get shipwrecked on an island, befriended by gypsies…but she has to return to save her country from the villainous Prime Minister, she leads her country to freedom and is crowned in the Cathedral…

HARRY: Well, splendid. I knew you had something ready. Of course, the Board will have to approve it, so can you let them have a synopsis tomorrow morning…

IFOR: …in the morning.…written out…?

HARRY: …as you've just outlined, remember?

IFOR: I can remember all of that, and more, word for word. Well! I will deliver a complete synopsis to you by ten tomorrow. I will go now, Harry, to write it up, copy it out…

HARRY: …you can send the completed script after the Board has met.

IFOR: …the rest of the story…

HARRY: …of course.

IFOR: Got it!

HARRY: And just one thing – the title…

IFOR: …well, that's the most difficult thing of all.

HARRY: You said it was 'glamorous'…

IFOR: …'Glamor' is a Welsh word. Means 'spell,' or 'enchantment.' So I am really an ancient princely Silurian under a spell from the Vale of Glamor…

HARRY: …and tonight you have proved it. The title?

IVOR: Flash! Yes, got it. Title, 'Glamorous Night!'

HARRY: Perfect!

IFOR: And I must have a free hand, in every decision.

HARRY: Alright, Ifor. But no 'me Tarzan!'stuff!

IFOR: Done! Mam's right, films are basically silly. One last thing! Most important of all. *(Shouts)* Waiter! Two Ivor Novello ice cream bombes, if you please.

(Fade lights they wait, heads together, talking rapidly. CUT LIGHTS AS WAITER arrives with ice creams)

ACT 2 SCENE 5

(IFOR'S Flat. Busy preparations for 'Glamorous Night.' Comings and goings. IFOR'S model theatre full of figures. Drawings of sets, costumes, on walls, samples of costumes, wigs, model of ocean liner. IVOR on phone, from time to time. EDDIE on second phone, doing Press, lots of photos; BOBBY checking drawings, lists, figures. KATIE ENTERS/EXITS, with drinks, bottles, sandwiches)

IFOR: Eddie, tell the Mail, the director of 'Glamorous Night' **is** Leontine Sagan, and yes, I am aware she is female, like my Mam, they're all over the place. Tell 'em that. Mam's part? Tell him to contact her direct. Good luck to him. And Katie. Lovely to see you again

KATIE: Lovely, Ifor. Like home.

BOBBY *(Holding up sketch of set, a court, crowded with figures)*: You here in just a blue suit, Ivor, side stage without the hussars and grandees?

IFOR: And in the last scene, Bobby, in my sweaty shirt sleeves, upstage right, in the shadow of the splendid court itself, and note, I do not sing a single note, but I shall be here, there, everywhere! My little theatre of dolls here has come to life at last! Note that, Eddie, for the slower Presses.

(PHONE RINGS. IFOR answers)

IFOR: Yes, this is the wardrobe, the dresser, the undresser, deviser, stage manager, so yes, check every costume, yes, all three hundred of them, one by one. Yes, there is no other way. Ring me back when you've finished. Fine. Go to it!

IFOR: My God, aren't we all so lucky, absolutely loving the things we're doing! Are the scripts delivered, Bobby.

BOBBY: No, they are not.

IFOR: Tell them to have the final copies here by three this afternoon, or its curtains. Unpunctuality is as bad as drink. And no drinking back stage, don't forget. Got all the moves blocked, Bobby?

BOBBY: Me and Leontine finished them last midnight. Ready to go.

IFOR: Good job as usual, and the set in the last scene, has it stopped swaying yet?

BOBBY: Carpenters onto it.

EDDIE *(On phone)*: 'The Times,' Ifor, how shall I headline it? - opera, operetta, musical play, drama - which?

IFOR: All of them! Call it my own special brand - 'Taff Unique!'

EDDIE *(On phone)*: Ifor, Mam just talked to The Evening Standard.

IFOR: I was wondering where she was.

EDDIE: As busy as you.

IFOR: What she up to?

EDDIE: She wants to put on an eisteddfod with her all Welsh Grandmother Choir - at the Albert Hall.

IFOR: Is that all? We're safe then.

EDDIE: She's always good copy but I've a feeling this is going to be big game.

IFOR: yes, Eddie! Digets, integers, figures, numerals, even the two times table, do not come into her understanding, Eddie.

BOBBY: 'Grandmothers' is right, I mean literally. Some of her choir are hanging on, but only just, due to Mam's often imaginary recitals and ignorance of simple arithmetic. She should retire, for her own sake.

IFOR: I agree. You agree. The world agrees…but… Katie tidy up here, my sheet music, please. We're off, down stage. Run through. No one in if they're late. You can come and watch later, Katie, if you want. If Mam calls, warn me! Off we go.

(EXEUNT BOBBY, EDDIE, KATIE, IFOR. ENTER CLARA furtively, front stage. Audience noises up. MAM tidies herself. Speaks in broad Welsh accent)

CLARA: Money is needed for my grand Jubilee recital to benefit Queen Alexandra's Field Nurse Fund, at the New Empire, Leicester Square, before royalty itself, for charity, see, my first retirement concert, see! So give generously. Look, see my hair. Why is it so lovely, you ask? Because I am an enthusiastic user of Evan William's marvellous 'shampoo *bleu.*' *(Holds up publicity circular, with her photo)* It's remarkable how, like, it preserves the natural beauty of my hair, now just showing little touches of gray. This! *(Holds up bottle)* Banish those yellowish tints! This magic elixir leaves hair looking slinky-like and brings its colour to the highest perfection. So young looking too, see. There's lovely. Hair, 'ordinary grade', cleanses and brightens, in white packets, six pence. There's lovely again. Hair, 'grade two', makes it sparkle with health, seven pence, in orange packets. There's lovely, as ever. And here the supreme 'shampoo bleu', for big bushes, blended for silvery cascades of locks. So natural. In aquamarine packets. Ten pence. That's top lovely there. Write to this Welsh magician of the coiffure, this brilliant Evan Williams, of Tonyryfail, send for his famous booklet on Fair Care for the Hair, now! Do it. For royalty. For charity. For you. For me!

(CUT LIGHTS to applause. ENTERS flat area. Lights up. Katie's peeps in, sees CLARA, withdraws. CLARA looks at drawings, sometimes disapproving. ENTER KATIE, IFOR behind her)

IFOR: Well, *(Pointing at cuttings)* Your statements to the Press, you been busy.

CLARA: No more'n you.

IFOR: Look what Eddie gave me this morning, report on your funny 'turn' last night at the Queen Elizabeth Rooms.

CLARA: I haven't had my picture on a poster for a whole year, Ifor.

IFOR: It says you were laughed off stage.

CLARA: I was laughed on stage.

IFOR: Why did you do it, Mam?

CLARA: It's only hair.

IFOR: Why?

CLARA: To pay the bills.

IFOR: But Eddie pays the bills.

CLARA: He's always trying to teach me arithmetic, a subject I've avoided all my life, you know that. It was the only thing I was not a prodigy at.

IFOR: Try to think in budgetary terms, that's all, Mam. The overall expenses. I mean, the chorus here for your next 'turn' at the Albert Hall – all little children, you know how difficult and expensive it is just to have one child on stage, but forty-two! - dressed variously as silver bees, purple beetles, rosy frogs, gilded may-flies, prancing unicorns, red dragons and green mermaids? Mam, that is not normal.

CLARA: Of course it is. I think in colossal terms. And Ifor, look at your next bit of fluff here. What have you got? An opera house, a ruined castle, lovers with real coronets, a mitred Bishop, a full Cathedral, a Swiss village, an avalanche, a liner shipwreck, a Mississippi showboat, Australian sheep, I ask you. And here, tossed into the bin, 'Lily of the Valley,' the great Welsh opera you're never going to write.

IFOR: It takes place in Tonypandy and I've roughed out the plot already.

CLARA: That and no more, no doubt.

IFOR: Mam, people pay to see my 'fluff', and all my bills are settled on the dot. That's half the fun.

CLARA: You've had tons of flops.

IFOR: And you've had no failures, have you, Mam?

CLARA: Well, glad you're right about something. And it's all catching up with me, age and all. My legs, look, a new one…

IFOR: …pardon?

CLARA: A new one, varicose veins, look.

IFOR: No thanks.

CLARA: Katie, help me to sit…I feel all faint…

IFOR: Come off it…

KATIE: …no, Ifor, the doctor warned her.

IFOR: Why didn't you tell me, Mam!? Here. *(Helps her to sit)*

CLARA: Thank you, Katie, you're back in the world now.

KATIE: I'll stay on, your Dad, wants us all to be friends and help each other. Easy to like. I am forgetting all past woes and bad conversations. Even with those rough boys. I turn a blind eye and a deaf ear to their mutterings. There are no complaints from me, bitterly spoken. Only the waters of the Thames, Ifor, so calm. Mam, you did it all for me, for us, for Ifor, for Dad. For kindness, famous you are, all over Wales…

CLARA: …all over the world…Yes, Ifor, the star, but second in the constellations, I was known in the Great Pavilions of the National Eisteddfod, don't forget that, an elected Bard of the Gorsedd, the throne of poets - my bardic name – 'Pencerddes Morganwg,' 'great Musician of Glamorgan,' and you remember, in 1905, when the town of Cardiff was granted 'City' status, I had a hand in that too, me and my royal brooch… (*Gasps in pain*) ah….

(KATIE Puts cushion behind her head)

IFOR: Katie, fetch the doctor.

(EXIT KATIE. MAM groans, clutches chest. IFOR agitated)

IFOR: Mam, Mam. Be … don't be ill…no, don't go, breathe, there, don't go, Mam, breathe deep, you do, best Mam in the world you are, love my Mam, please don't go, stay, for just a minute, you'll be alright, don 't go, don't leave me…

(MAM is lying, face to audience. IfOR's face upstage on her shoulder, MAM'S face not visible to him)

I swear, please God, I will always look after you Mam, no questions, I promise, and you will not ever want for a penny in future, I will pay every bill, without question, for you're my lovely Mam, I swear it.

(One of mam's eyes snaps open, she smiles into audience. Winks. Footsteps on stairs. IFOR strokes CLARA'S hand. ENTER KATIE and DOCTOR. CUT LIGHTS)

ACT 2 SCENE 6
(Months later. IFOR'S Flat. CLARA and IFOR, sitting by phone)
IFOR: He'll be alright, Doctor said it was just his dropsy again.
CLARA: I always told him to go for walks, even do my breathing exercises. They would have helped. But he wouldn't listen. He'd just sit there…
IFOR: …enjoying us, our best audience. Good old Dad.
CLARA: Most popular man at the office.
IFOR: We should go down to Redroofs I think Mam.
CLARA: You've got a matinee, Ifor
IFOR: It's our Dad, Mam.
CLARA: I know. Dad would understand, like he'll be sitting in the back row of the stalls, enjoying your latest triumph. He'll be there. As I would be.
(Phone rings. MAM jumps at it. Listens, sobs, slumps onto IFOR'S shoulder. IFOR takes phone. Listens)
CLARA: He's gone, Ifor. Gone. Our dear Dad.
IFOR *(Listens)*: 'Thrombosis,' 'dropsy.' Yes, I understand. Yes, Doctor. Where to? Mam?
CLARA: Hearse to Harrod's, then Golder's Green Crematorium. Dad got it all arranged.
IFOR: We'll be coming down directly, Doctor. Thank you. Goodbye. He went very quietly, Mam, no pain.

Doctor's preparing him. All in order, even his papers by his bedside table, Doctor said.

CLARA: Only this morning, having breakfast with him, in bed, holding his hand.

(Strokes IFOR'S hand. CLARA sobs. They embrace. Cut LIGHTS)

ACT 2 SCENE 7

(IFOR'S Flat. Years later. EDDIE, BOBBY, IFOR discuss business)

EDDIE: Well, Ifor, at last – first night is 'Glamorous Night'!

IFOR: Bless you, again. Helped so much. My friends. Dear as Dad. Mam's not over it, as much as she can be, she says. Katie's such a help, staying on. But Mam's plotting again, swears she's still rearin' to go. Where she gets her energy, I don't know, but where she gets her hope is an even bigger puzzle. She will carry on…

BOBBY: …**you** carried on.

IFOR: Keep going – I hope.

EDDIE: That's it.

BOBBY: We've got the up-to-date sums here…

IFOR: …my five-year Bobby-business-sandwich.

EDDIE: And the percentages…

IFOR: …down to the last farthing,

BOBBY: No loose ends…

IFOR: …or loose cash!

EDDIE: '32, a good year, three plays as actor writer, double the fee; thirty three, better, four plays again with you on stage in each… check this list, Ifor, films, 'Once a Lady,' 'The Lodger' ' I Iived with you…' yes, 'Autumn Crocus'… in the correct sequence!

IFOR: A feat! Thanks again, lad.

EDDIE: Royalties from all your songs, the old review numbers too. They're steady. 'Home Fires' tops the list. And after that, it gets amazing! 'Murder in Mayfair,'…

IFOR: Huh! They loved it, I did not. *(Looks through papers)* And wages, payments, outgoings, Mam again, I see…

EDDIE: 12,000 pounds, Ifor.

IFOR: I wish it was double. Really, I haven't quite found the shapes, sounds and stories I want, all together in one mind, so to speak; still just popular fragments, and my film days are drawing to a close, not that I mind going out as Tarzan, The Ape Man. No, all my dreams and hopes now are for Glamorous Night. And why? because I have real control over the imaginings, the inventions, the music, direction, set, spectacle, song which means, **everything** - so that I have no whit of an excuse for any error whatsoever, however slight, and I can fly free as a feather in the wind - to what end? We'll see! Thanks my friends again, you are life to me. And the orchestra is still playing!

ACT 2 SCENE 8

(Dark back stage. Spot on NEWSVENDOR holding headline shet, newspapers under arm.. NEWSVENDOR accent from cockney to posh. Faint snatches of IVOR'S Songs from theatre)

NEWSVENDOR *(Cockney):* Read all about it! Read all about it! Five hundred years later, or so, and still here! Read all about it! *(Points backstage, name 'Glamorous Night' comes up in lights.)* There! Triumph of 'Glamorous Night!' You bet, mate! 'Cheers, shouts and yells, for Ivor and a tornado of clapping.' That's wot I said and done and I stands by it. What else? *(Posh accent)* 'It is unsparingly, intoxicatingly, wildly triumphant.' Blimey, lots of words but not much

meaning! 'He has devised a superb entertainment, a complete new departure, his own unique invention.' 'It all illustrates the tremendous range of the composer. They have never had anything like this at Drury Lane or anywhere else. Only a superb theatre craftsman could have brought this off.' 'If as some say, it is all punk, then it is inspired punk!' *(Cockney)* 'I takes me hat off to him, like the rest of us, mate! 'He has here built up the highest achievement of his career.' I seconds that. And them many achievement is now called 'The Bobby Sandwich' and it stands higher than Nelson's bleeding column, mate, and it's still growing! Next show, 'Careless Rapture!' I heard. The reviews? Ditto, mate, as above! And 'The Dancing Years! *(He points. The Dancing Years' comes up in lights) (Posh)* 'There is no composer for the theatre who can give us such pleasant music, tuneful and tender.' *(Cockney)* Down with Mr Hitler and all 'is doodlebugs, is what Ifor is saying this time. No one can stop music. On with 'The Dancing Years' for us all. And more to come, he told me, 'Perhaps to Dream'; and the 'King's Delight' or words like that, don't miss it, got my tickets booked already. *(Shouts in cockney)* Triumphs for Novello! Never grow old! Read all about it! Read all about it.
(FADE SOUNS)

ACT 2 SCENE 9
(IFOR'S Flat. Hot Summer's evening. BOBBY, IFOR, EDDIE sunbathing, walk in and out of terrace)
IFOR: Right, I still think 'Dancing Years' is my best to date, although there are always large areas in which I can improve.
BOBBY: I doubt it, Ivor, one hit-show after another, 'Glamorous Night' kicked it off, then 'Careless Rapture,' 'Crest of the Wave,' now 'The Dancing Years,'

pulling in the masses. HM Tennent in raptures too. Full houses at Drury Lane. 'Read all about it,' as the papers say.

IFOR: And although it's about Mr Hitler and his treatment of the Jews, it is still not a 'political play,' it is about the ultimate victory of music. I believe in the theatre, in the beauty of the theatre, I want to give people a chance to dream, I want to show them the Land of Might Have Been…

BOBBY: '…and mother came too.'

IFOR: I know people say, 'old Ifor just churns out the stuff.' Well, if it's so easy let them have a go! They'd go stark staring mad in five minutes! I mean, look at me! I only write like I'm an old bolster bursting with feathers straining to get out. And when they do, whoooosh! Watch out!

EDDIE: The High Priest of the Spectacular is on the air!

IFOR: This is the thing, and it is no secret just an obvious truth - if you can convince the audience that they do not exist, they'll never take their eyes off you! True, try it. But let's get down to earth; you've know Mam's new 'spectacular? - grand tour of the Continent with 'sixty of her girls, took the Jewish question in 'The Dancing Years' a bit too seriously, bless her. Her and her Welsh Grandmothers, what was left of them, on a planned tour starting at the Hague, going on to Belgium, then Nuremberg and finishing in Berlin, to perform her folk songs before Hitler himself, with a grand finale of a thousand doves released over the Berlin stadium, all carrying on their tiny legs, messages of peace. 'Love. Not war!' 'It was' she wrote to me, 'the greatest triumph of my life!' And I think it was. Although it never happened. Her 'peace drive' was all in the mind, and nothing wrong with that. This to save the Jews and stop the war was the aim of all her publicity. For others. Isn't that glorious! But panic messages as soon as she started off, bookings cancelled, debts mounting, fell asleep on the train, lost her way, forgot the addresses of the hotels, some of the grandmas even deserted and went home. Don't worry, still fit as a fiddle, carryng on 'for both herself and Dad,' she said. Fast asleep at Redroofs I left her. She'll be in her Royal Box at Drury Lane when my next is launched, given a war or two. And let me warn you, she is now writing her autobiography. And she's found a publisher, I copied this out of the first few pages, 'My life comes from the rich soil of Glamorgan. My Welsh ancestors lived among nature's wonders and walked with God, talking to him in their everyday lives as a matter of course, in rain, storm and sunshine…I not only taught my students how to sing but also the knowledge of how to live… I hope!" God bless her all over again!

EDDIE: The crowned Queen of First Nights!

(ALL EXIT to Terrace. Sound of planes overhead, air raid sirens, searchlights criss-cross)

ACT 2 SCENE 10
(IFOR'S FLAT. BOBBY, IFOR, piles of papers, documents on desk. IVOR in HENRY V armour. HENRY V's helmet, sword, gauntlets, on table)
IFOR: All tidy when Katie's here.
BOBBY: Like a sister.
IFOR: Yes...
EDDIE: And you really want to play this Henry V?
IFOR: 'Once more unto the breach…!' Know the words already. Try the helmet here. See the visor comes down.
(Puts on helmet, pulls down visor, puts on catch, makes a few passes with sword. All laugh. IFOR tries to tug off helmet. It sticks. IFOR pulls hard. Helmet stuck)

BOBBY: The catch is stuck. Here. *(IFOR sruggles)*

IFOR *(Muffled, visor down)*: Hey, get me out of in here!
(EDDIE, BOBBY struggle to pull off helmet)

EDDIE: Need soap.

BOBBY: Good idea. Wet it first.

(EXIT EDDIE. RE-ENTERS with dripping bar of soap. They soap IFOR'S neck, and tug. Soap again, Tug. Helmet flies off with bar of soap. All tumble down, look at each other, laughing, rolling on the ground. IFOR chases them with sword)

IFOR: 'We band of brothers!'

EDDIE: A great victory has blessed your arms, Prince Ifor!

IFOR: For St George and Merry Wales!

BOBBY: A short reign but a funny one!

(Tidy themselves up. IFOR spots envelope)

IFOR: Don't like the look of that one*! (Tears open envelope)* Blast, Bobby, turned down my application for supplementary petrol coupons again. How am I supposed to get to Redwoods from here. No petrol, but you can buy caviar at the Savoy down the road.

BOBBY: All part of the war effort.

IFOR: Whose, I'm beginning to wonder. Will you drive me down?

(BOBBY hears shouts outside from Terrace.)

BOBBY: Hang on, was that my name?

(EXIT to Terrace. KNOCK on Flat main door, right back)

IFOR: Come in.

(ENTER DOORMAN hesitantly, in uniform, touches cap)

DOORMAN: I been waiting. Didn't want to disturb, Ifor.

IFOR: That's quite alright, Tom. How can I help you?

DOORMAN: I got one of your top fans outside

IFOR: Really. Which one?

DOORMAN: 'Dora,' she said.

IFOR: Yes, I know her, a faithful follower. Got to be kind for our fans. Show her in.

(EXIT DOORMAN RE-ENTERS with DORA, thirty-five, adores IFOR. Carries programmes of Ifor shows)

DORA: It's wonderful you seeing me like this. I've seen you 220 times on stage, Mr Novello. Thank you so much. If you could sign these…

IFOR *(Signing programmes)*: …we all adore our fans, Dora, without you, where would we be?

DORA: Excuse me, I couldn't help hearing out there, the problem you've got with cars to take you home after the theatre. Well, if I could suggest something, I work for the Electrical and General Industrial Trust, quite a mouthful, but I could arrange to transfer your Rolls onto our roster and apply for a license under 'Work of national Importance.'

IFOR: You could do that?

DORA: I am the Chief Secretary of the Company, sir, I mean, ' Ifor.'

IFOR: How?

DORA: I'll need all the documents, ownership, registration certificates and all that.

IFOR: Wonderful! Tom, take this angel down to the car, my out-of-work driver will be there, instruct him to give all documents to Dora here.

DORA: They'll be returned later.

IFOR: When can I use the car?

DORA: As from tomorrow, Ifor, I'll give the transfer top priority.

IFOR: Thank you, darling girl!

(Kisses her. DORA EXITS with DOORMAN. RE-ENTER Bobby)

BOBBY: Who was that?

IFOR: An angel in the shape of a fan.

BOBBY: Good stuff! One of my fans too, told me I was the best dainty devil dancer in Mandarin costume she'd ever seen!

IFOR: The first of thousands!

BOBBY: I'll drive you down…

IFOR:…nooo…I've come to an arrangement, full use of Mr Rolls! Wonderful.

BOBBY: … but what about the blitz?

IFOR: As an experienced aviator, I can tell you it's failed. But watch out for these new doodle-bug things, not much to stop them at the moment. And 'places of entertainment' all open again in spite of the bombs and blackouts. Rolls back in action! Can't tell you how relieved I am. I've drawn up my itinerary, Bobby, Troop Concerts *(Hands him paper)* Gun batteries, drill halls, canteens, barracks, depots, front lines…

BOBBY: '…front lines'? - they won't let you near those.

IFOR: 'Home Fires' all over again.

IVOR: I'm polishing up a new one this time too, Bobby, 'We'll Gather Lilacs in the Spring again…' Soon be ready. Premiere it over there.

BOBBY: You'll follow the troops?

IFOR: When the beachheads are established, I'll be there. And now the fate of 'The Dancing Years,' the 'Prancing Years' I call them, 'Careless Rupture's the name of the game! Drury Lane have agreed. After the tour we will re-launch the ocean liner there.

BOBBY: I should think so! One hundred per cent capacity! Will the Queen of First nights be well enough to take her box?

IFOR: She seems to be taking the war seriously at last, Bobby, she's fallen asleep. Katie's visiting us, so It's Welsh all the way. Cheers her up, yr hen iaith, the old language. Know what the Queen said to me last night? – 'if Hitler had only heard my choir of Welsh Ladies, this hideous war would never have happened.' And I have no illusions about my age, drawing on now – how I hate that expression – so many 'drawing ons' –tougher as the years go by, but I promise I'll take it easy, in Venice or Montego Bay, with you, as always…

BOBBY: …and your thirty thousand friends. Can't wait. By the way your new loud-speaker system is installed.

IFOR: Thank you, Bobby, lad. Now they can not only read the takings in my dressing room mirror in greasepaint, now it will be announced all over the theatre as well!

BOBBY: The Board of Management won't like it.

IFOR: I want everyone to share in the fun. I want everyone to share in the profit.

BOBBY: Eddie's latest figures here, your take, seven and a half per cent up to three thousand five hundred, and after that, ten per cent. With fees for writer, composer, devisor, total comes to over twenty per cent of the gross.

IFOR: Disgusting. Leave it to me! I'll fix it. Do you know, my greatest pleasure now, to look around at one of my parties, and to see that out of forty guests, I have known thirty of them for over twenty years. From my old cook to HM Tennent himself!

BOBBY: And the great Garbo says, for posterity, that a party at Redwoods is the only place in England she ever wants to be.

(Phone rings. IFOR answers)

IFOR: Katie! Hello. *(He listens)* No, no, no, no…

(BOBBY helps IFOR to sit, takes receiver)

BOBBY: Hello, Katie. What's happened? Definite? Thrombosis. Yes, my dear, seventy nine. Yes, we'll take care of it. Put on the Doctor. *(Listens)* Yes, make out the certificate. Same arrangements as for David. Harrod's. Yes, Golder's Green Crematorium. I'll confirm it. Yes, Ifor's here. Yes. Thank you, Doctor. Katie, you there? Look, stay. Help the doctor. Sit with Mam. See you later. Goodbye.

IFOR: Mam, Mam! (*Sobs*) What a thing, Bobby. Mam. Gone. I don't know what to do! I tried for her, I tried. Always grandchildren. My best, not enough. Mam, Mam, I'm sorry…I'm coming... *(Makes to leave.)*

BOBBY: …no, sit down. Listen now, Ifor, you can't leave your people here, you can't leave her down there...

IFOR: …I know, I know…

BOBBY: … which is it to be?

IFOR: What she would have done herself.

BOBBY: Mam never let an audience down.

IFOR: Yes. Yes. Help me prepare, got thirty minutes.

BOBBY: You've made her happy.

IFOR: I only ever tried, my Bobby.

BOBBY: That's it. *(Voices from below)* Listen. Sounds like a full house too.

(In mirror, BOBBY fondly helps IFOR make up. As LIGHTS FADE, SOUND of solitary doodle bug overhead. CUT LIGHTS, SOUND)

ACT 2 SCENE 11

(IFOR'S Flat. Night. KATIE, IFOR talk. Subdued. KATIE dressed for traveling, suitcase close by. Tour photos on walls hand in hand. IFOR points to photo as Henry V)

IFOR: There I am Katie, my King to Mam's Queen.

KATIE: Why did they take it off?

IFOR: The War.

KATIE: All them bombs.

IFOR: One went straight through the roof here and smashed into the stalls. Didn't go off. But my Henry V did. Bomb's still on display, top balcony corridor, I am not!

KATIE (*reads from cutting by photo*): 'Novello played the part most graciously. The best speeches were the quiet ones. Most impressive.' I should think so too! Lovely you were.

(*She strokes Ifor's hand*)

KATIE: Mam. She brought me back to the world, she did.

IFOR: And she brought me into the world too, Katie.

KATIE: What a lovely life she had, just what she wanted.

IFOR: 'The life I Loved,' she called it. Thanks for the lilac tree.

KATIE: All the old choir chipped in, who was left of them.

IFOR: Over Mam and Dad's ashes, it will bloom white.

KATIE: And for your song about lilacs.

IFOR: Not finished yet.

KATIE: You are going on, aren't you, Ifor?

IFOR: I have a new idea which seems to be finding room somewhere. Yes, I'll be going on.

KATIE: Why… all-white here, Ifor?

IFOR: So I can fill every space.

KATIE: Before I go, can I put up my favourite pictures? Yours. Ours. l know where they are.

(*Opens drawer, pins up the two photos in Act 1 Sc 1, from Sandy Wilson's 'Ivor' (page 108)*)

KATIE: There's lovely you are, Ifor.

IFOR: 'Twice,' as Mam used to say.

KATIE: Thank you, God. (*They embrace*) Like a sister to us, you are. Now I'd like you to do one last thing for me. Here…(*Takes out MAM'S 'royal' brooch*) I want you to have this - yes, the next generation. For you, for your Mam, for all Mam's choir Ladies of Wales. 'Imperatrix.' Put it here. *(Puts it on table)* If you could call all the Ladies together, all who're left, to meet in Sion Chapel, in Cathays, where Mam and Dad were married, and put this on the Big Seat for all to see. Then sit the Ladies around like we're sitting now, Katie, and you lead them in a choice of Mam's favourite hymns and songs, 'Cymru Fydd', 'Wales for ever!' 'Yr Deryn Pur,' 'O gentle dove!' 'We'll Gather Lilacs,' some of my own if you like, so all the angels above will hear and know that our lovely Mam has arrived, the selfsame Creator of the Ladies Choir of Wales, conducted by Madame Clara Novello Davies, our Mam, in person up there at the Pearly gates she always knew were there and are now opening for her.

KATIE: I will, I will.

(IFOR pins brooch on Katie. They embrace, sobbing. CUT LIGHTS)

ACT 2 SCENE 12:

(Flat, IFOR pacing, looking at pictures. Knock on door. ENTER DOORMAN, hands IFOR a brown envelope)

DOORMAN: Sorry to interrupt, says 'urgent,' Ifor.

IFOR: Thanks, Tom.

DOORMAN: Anything I can do.

IFOR: If only. Thanks.

(EXIT TOM. IFOR opens envelope. Stares)

IFOR: A.... summons? What on earth is this?

(Dials phone)

IFOR: Bobby. Listen, I've got a summons. *(Looks at docs)* Says 'to appear at Bow Street Magistrates' Court...to answer charges relating to....conspiracy to commit an act against the Motor Restriction Order 1942'...what does that mean, Bobby? I've done nothing illegal. *(Listens)* Yes, that was Dora, the Secretary to the Company. Come over, Bobby, tell Eddie to come too. One damn thing after another. Ta, love you.

ACT 2 SCENE 13

(SPOT ON NEWSVENDOR side stage)

NEWSVENDER: Read all about it. Ifor Novello arrested. Now in court. Charges laid. Novello in court today. Read all about it!

(Fade to sounds as in court, Sound of a gavel)

VOICE OF JUDGE: The Novello case, is it, Clerk of the Court? Theatre vagabonds, far too many, and he's one of those, too, most unhealthy.

VOICE OF CLERK OF THE COURT: Be uprising for his Honour, Judge Mackenna. Next, Case 40, Novello versus the Crown.

(Lights Up. JUDGE, at bench, in robes, a parody of Punch, sits, glaring at IFOR in dock. Whispers behind hand to CLERK)

JUDGE: So this is Novello, well, not for long in this Court. My summary will be brief. *(Addresses Court)* The transfer of the motor car in question, was the work of one, Grace Walton, alias Dora Constable. She was not 'Secretary to the Company' as she described herself but a mere clerk in the typing pool of the said company. She has confessed to this deception, which she said was due to her adoration of Mr Novello and that he used this to her detriment. *(Aside)* Certainly most ungentlemanly. She admitted following him around many times, making a nuisance of herself…

IFOR: …no, your Honour, a fan is never a nuisance

JUDGE: Silence in Court! To continue - she also complains that Mr Novello is putting all the onus of guilt onto her, and claims this is most unfair. Constable Blake also stated that Mr Novello had once suggested that 'the whole affair should be kept secret.' But this is hearsay and unacceptable. In answer to the assertion that Mr Novello had bribed her with a pair of earrings, Mr Novello pointed out that the value of the earrings was only one pound or so, and that this hardly constituted 'bribery.' But this cannot be dismissed out of hand. Grace Walton also claimed that Mr Novello had 'actually produced one of her plays' and 'would do anything crooked to get his car on the road again.' But these assertions proved to be mere fantasy. Her Petrol Inspector when questioned admitted that 'Dora,' or 'Grace' had no authority to arrange any of these transfers and that her superiors had no idea that any such false transactions had actually taken place. It was only due to the vigilance of the Petrol Board that fuel discrepancies were noticed and further enquiries carried out. Mr Novello pleaded that he only agreed to the arrangement because he believed it to be 'absolutely bona fida.' But, I ask you, is that not incredible? It is impossible to believe that Mr Novello didn't know exactly what he was doing. This whole fraud was a subterfuge to get around the Motor Restrictions Act, a flagrant breach of the law. Although Miss Grace Walton has proved herself an inveterate liar, the burden of guilt rests with Mr Novello. Miss Walton is hereby dismissed with a fine of fifty pounds. However, Mr Novello is found guilty and I hereby sentence him to a term of two months in prison, with costs! Appeal granted if you wish. Take him down.

(Bangs gavel. Fade court whispers and voices)

ACT 2 SCENE 14

(Prison call, Wormwood Scrubs. Small, table, chairs, papers, toilet bucket in corner, sound of pissing. Clang of steel doors, echoing footsteps, keys jangling, dim

light through bars of small window. IFOR lying on bed in prison uniform. Ghost of MAM appears by window, in flowery dress, her brooch gleaming, waving her golden baton IFOR rises, holding out arms)

IFOR: Mam! Mam! Forgive me! Mam. Don't come. Don't see me. Don't go! Let you down, all. Friends family. I am not here. Don't go. Not here! Help Mam, help.

(IFOR reaches out his arms, MAM dissolves. Sound of snores, grunts, cries, mutterings. Bell rings for reveille. Lights up. IFOR crouches by bed. On table pile of mail bags, with heavy thread, needles, IVOR'S 'job.' Ifor looks at pile of mail bags, gazes in pain at hands, raw and bleeding. He tries to sew, stabs himself with needle, cries out, weeps silently on all fours on floor, groaning, holding head. Clang, sound of keys as WARDER enters, with tray of porridge, bunch of mail bags)

WARDER: Wakey, wakey! Come on, Inmate Novello, six-thirty! Breakfast. Eat up!

(IFOR takes tray. Tries food, spits it out, gags)

WARDEN: You get no more till midday. *(Of mail bags)* Here's your lot for today.

(Dumps mailbags on table)

IFOR: My hands…bleeding…I can't…

WARDEN: You'll do your quota like everyone else. You'll get used to it. Leave it then. Where's your bucket? *(Looks inside)* Blimey, not enough for a mouse. Take your bucket when you hear the whistle, doors open, you step outside, line up with the rest. Take your bucket and slop it into the latrine. *(IFOR sniffs bucket, gags)* Don't worry. And the mail bags…

IFOR: …but my hands…

WARDER: …they'll harden up…

IFOR: …but I'm a pianist…

WARDER: Can't help that. All the same here. Padre's visiting you soon. Moved you from downstairs...

IFOR: ...murderers, thieves, rapists...why did they put me in there?

WARDER: ...like I said, not on this floor. You don't know how lucky you are.

IFOR: Did my Mam visit me?

WARDER: What?

IFOR: I saw my Mam, over there, conducting her Ladies. *(Does MAM'S vocal exercises, conducts)* The Great Deliverer.

(ENTER PADRE, with books, sheet music)

WARDER *(Aside to Padre, of IFOR)*: Bit round the twist if you asks me, Padre.

PADRE: Leave it to me, Bill.

WARDER: Cheers, then.

(EXIT WARDER)

IFOR: Padre. At last. Every second is torture here. Not the filthy food, or the regime, or the slop out, but the failure. I've let down all my friends...family. My Mam. Padre, I saw her.

WARDER: So did I.

IFOR: You did!? My Mam? Where was it?

PADRE: After the Appeal you were brought straight here.

IFOR: Memory is patchy. Should I have pleaded guilty and thrown myself on the mercy of the Court?

PADRE: You wouldn't have got any mercy out of Magistrate McKenna, he's a hanging judge. Well known.

IFOR: Why?

PADRE: He hates all theatre folk, male and female, in his patch, especially the more...sensitive types...

IFOR: Thanks for telling me. Your accent. Where are you from?

PADRE: Cardiff.

IFOR: Where?

PADRE: Cathays. Padre Morgan.

IFOR: God bless you!

(Embraces PADRE)

IFOR: Mam. You saw her, you say?

PADRE: In the Jubilee Rooms, by the Town Hall.

IFOR: Cardiff! Marvellous! Not so alone now.

PADRE: You have less than a month to go.

IFOR: But my hands…

PADRE: …your friends have been active on your behalf.

IFOR: I am doubly blessed then.

PADRE: I've just come from the Governor's Office. You are hereby taken off the mailbag duty, and appointed assistant librarian…

IFOR: …the library?!

PADRE: …where I am to take you now and in future. But first, you must slop out…

IFOR: …of course.

PADRE: …and eat, keep your strength up. You're all skin and bones, Mr Novello.

IFOR: 'Ifor' please. *(Points at porridge)* I can't eat that.

PADRE: Your friends have sent a hamper… the Governor, you see, doesn't want a famous corpse on his hands…

IFOR: …or a raving madman.

PADRE: I told him I knew what you needed.

IFOR: You did? And what was that?

PADRE: Music paper to write on, to conduct from, a baton, here, and above all, a choir.

IFOR: A choir? Where from? Heaven?

PADRE: Earth. The prison choir.

IFOR: Excellent. And what do you need for it?

PADRE: A composer, a conductor and an accompanist.

IFOR: Have you got a piano?

PADRE: An old upright,

IFOR: We'll see about that.

PADRE: But it can still carry a tune.

IFOR: I thought I heard an organ.

PADRE: That was me, in the Chapel, where the choir are now assembled waiting for their new Choir Master.

IFOR: Marvellous! What do they think of me now, the base Novello?

PADRE: What everyone else thinks - gross miscarriage of justice. You're McKenna's latest victim, a scapegoat. They hate that little devil. Look at that Grace woman, walks free with a fine, and you one month on appeal, and as for petrol, it's sold on street corners practically. So welcome, Maistro Novello, martyr to the law, servant to music and hero to the people!

IFOR: Mam came to tell me all this, Padre.

PADRE: I'm sure she did. Now, the choir, I have to put up an official 'justification', which is 'education' in this case. Some of the choir are illiterate. I've worked out a scheme where you can 'supervise,' cut outs from all the magazines, I've got a pile ready, and to teach them to read from the pictures. The rest is song. What do you say?

IFOR: God bless you, that is why I am here, so I **can** say that, and help the others as I needed help from you and my friends. Thank you... *(Brushes himself down)* Got to look good for my fellow felons…

PADRE: … fans

(Flapping of wings at window)

IFOR: What's that?

PADRE: The pigeons…

IFOR: …of course, it's breakfast time! Here. *(Pushes out plate of porridge on window sill)* Cooo, coooo… *(Picks up a pigeon, cuddles it)* A cuddle, then. See, Padre, it's happy now, like me.

(CUT LIGHTS)

ACT 2 SCENE 15

(IFOR'S Flat. BOBBY, IFOR; IFOR paces, very pale, voraciously eating a dish of cold rice pudding. IFOR half dressed for stage)

IFOR: Mm, mmm, manna from heaven, like mother made, best rice pudding in the world, only food I miss. What's the time?

BOBBY: An hour before curtain up.

IFOR: My stand-in's done a fantastic job, I'll find him another part.

BOBBY: Audience is waiting for the return of their hero. Friends are waiting in the front rows.

IFOR: What do they think of Ifor now? Bobby, I've never felt so nervous about going on stage.

BOBBY: Your stand-in's waiting for a word from you.

IFOR: I felt like Marie Antoinette fleeing the mob.

BOBBY: And your new legal Rolls is waiting to take you to the party afterwards.

IFOR: I see you painted out all the arrow signs.

BOBBY: Out there, while you were away, played to full houses every night. And Queen Mary's booked seats again for later.

IFOR: Then Mam will be there as well in the box. I saw her inside, you know. I did not distress her.

BOBBY: The show went on,

IFOR: And does so still. Bless you, Mam, deliverer! From the first circle of hell to the last rays of hope. If I've learned anything, Bobby, from all this, it is to cherish the rice pudding moments of life and make sure to share them with friends.

BOBBY: And after this long run is over, there's your new 'King's Rhapsody' to get into some kind of running order. 'Will Ifor never stop?!' - they're all asking again.

IFOR: You ask it so well, Bobby, I feel better already. But look at me. What am I built for now?

BOBBY: To make music, to have fun.

IFOR: In spite of my hollow chest, spindly legs! I can still hardly believe that I completed my sentence only yesterday at midnight. Me, the Prancing Queen.

BOBBY: What do I say to the stand-in?

IFOR: Get my blue suit ready!

BOBBY: Only one hour to prepare.

IFOR: Done it before.

(BOBBY looks out of terrace)

BOBBY: They're coming, and in hords, full house again by the look of it. Come on! 'On stage!' Ifor Novello!

(EXIT BOBBY, IFOR, arm in arm. CUT LIGHTS, SILENCE. Bursts of cheers, applause. 'For He's a Jolly Good Fellow' rises in chorus. SPOT on IFOR front stage, in blue suit, addressing audience)

IFOR: 'This has been the most exciting and wonderful thing that has ever happened to me. I have always known of your great kindness to me as a player, but tonight I feel it is kindness to me as a person. I have to say that in the last few weeks and especially with you tonight, I have been raised up again by the fondness of my friends here, I have been inspired by the balm of the music of your voices in the air, and enriched by the love of family present and past, Mam, Dad, and Katie. I shall try to convey these feelings of joy and affection to you in my next musical passage with time, 'King's Rhapsody.' See you there again on the first night! I thank you, with all my heart! Thank you. Thank you.

(Huge cheers, 'For he's a Jolly Good Fellow…' FADE as IFOR bows. CUT LIGHTS)

ACT 2 SCENE 16

(The Flat. BOBBY, EDDIE, IFOR, drinking Champagne)

IFOR: If I died at this very moment, it would be in the knowledge that a bad prison Choir can sometimes sound sweeter than a full philharmonic orchestra. I believe that all inhumanity comes from the futile black boredom of prison cells of any kind, with no hope of release, or family or friends. Isolation, total. I know that Mam will never leave me and will always sit in that Royal Box of hers till my dying day. God, I'm spouting like a real fool today. Now, Eddie, business. You've got my list. Just check it off. A new piano for the Scrubs, with a new organ, the cost being a pleasure, and a piano for Holloway and the ladies as well. Regular free tickets for my shows to the Warders and inmates, with special box for Padre Morgan of Cathays and his Mam when they visit any of my shows. And light entertainment for the inmates once a month. Reviews, Music Hall. Nothing solemn. And bless them all.

EDDIE: What about this tour of the Front. You feel up to it?

IFOR: I did it last war, I'll do it this one.

BOBBY: They won't let you near the fighting.

IFOR: I shall do the best whatever they offer me.

BOBBY: More music?

IFOR: No. This time a straight whodunnit, get their mind off things. 'Love from a Stranger,' that will do it. Got the scripts here. Small cast, no big sets, no costumes, no lorries, just a car for the actors. Launch at Bayeux, Normandy.

BOBBY: We are advancing on all fronts.

EDDIE: Now, are you sure you're up to it?

IFOR: I promise you.

BOBBY: You need to get back your normal weight, Ifor.

IFOR: Really, I will.

BOBBY: An eight week tour. Four shows a day sometimes?

IFOR: I can do it. But no porridge!

BOBBY: Just one last thing, that when the play finishes, you give a rendering of 'Home Fires…'

IFOR: …excellent idea! And I'll premiere my new song there too, 'We'll Gather Lilacs in the Spring again…'

EDDIE: Brilliant! 'Fires' for the grandfathers, 'Lilacs' for the sons!

IFOR: To remind them of the bliss of Hope. Our essential War Work, with or without petrol!

BOBBY: See this *(Holds up newspaper clipping)*: Obituary notice. 'Magistate H. MacKenna. Sterling services to Law. Deceased. Thrombosis.

IFOR: May his remains burn in – Golder's Green Crematorium!

(Toast, cheer. IFOR plays 'Lilacs' on piano)

ACT 2 SCENE 17

(IFOR'S Flat. A year later. IFOR dictates his will into tape)

IFOR: 'yes…' *(Stops tape)* Yes, Montego Bay property sold and put into Ivor Novello Trust. Personal cash gifts to friends, as listed. How much have I got left? 156,000 pounds have got to go. First Bobby, 22,000 and the property, Redroofs, with all furniture, plus my jewellery and objets d'art. Mam's collection of amber and rose quartz, for dear Katie. Cash legacies, as listed, to my staff, Eddie, and my driver, dresser, the doormen, and clerks. The pensioners I supported to continue to receive payments, chauffeur, cook. No paymets to me for mortgages undertaken, further payment cancelled on the day of my death. To the Pension Fund for Actors, the Actor's Orphanage, Actors' Benevolent Fund, RADA,

grants for Ivor Novello scholarships, four thousand pounds, as listed. Royalties from 'The 'Dancing Years' to my dear Godson, Tom Arnold, part of the family. All outstanding personal debts to be forgiven. My body I direct to be collected by Harrod's Funeral Parlour and delivered for cremation at Golder's Green, my ashes to lie next to my dearest Mam and Dad. Given this day 1950…There. The cupboard should be bare now. All under Ivor Novello Charities Ltd.
(CUT LIGHTS)

ACT 2 SCENE 18

(A year later. The Flat. Piles of cuttings, newspapers, reviews. BOBBY, EDDIE, IFOR talking. IVOR bronzed)

EDDIE: Must say Montego Bay cheered you up. But…

IFOR: …ate like a horse. Made no difference. Behold the ten-stone weakling!

EDDIE: 'King's Rhapsody' still playing to full houses, even with these new American musicals. *(Reads)* 'Not even Rogers and Hammerstien or Cole Porter can beat this.' 'Since Oklamhoma we've been in a coma and no one wants us' except Ifor Novello!

BOBBY: These reviews, best ever I'd say, and that's saying something!

IFOR: I think, all in all, it's the best piece I've ever written.

BOBBY: Practically every song a hit, and 'Gather Lilacs' over the moon!

EDDIE: Royalties a thousand a week. Amazing! Sheet music and scores sold out in the foyer after every performance.

BOBBY: '…alive with vitality, shamelessly enjoyable, of great value, represents real poetry for the masses.'

BOBBY: But listen to Noel, '…stinking with bad taste, intermixed with the basic vulgarity of Novello. The lead actress was outstanding, but what horrible stuff she had to say. All received rapturously, of course.'

IFOR: Poor Noel. Send him the best Magnum of Champagne from Harrods. That should bring a smile to his lips

BOBBY (*Reading):* 'How does Novello do it? And the answer, 'It doesn't matter as long as he carries on doing it!'

EDDIE: And the receipts are all on our side. And listen to Noel again. '…it is the very acne of vulgarity to write the receipts up on his dressing room mirror.'

IFOR: Noel is quite right. In future I shall write them up on the big mirror in the foyer! *(ALL cheer)* And the Queen was in the Royal box…

BOBBY: …her Majesty loved it.

IFOR: Bless you, Mam. Really, the Land of Illusion is the only real world I know. Above all, my loves, I am a sort of betwixt and between and if there ever was a hymn that was neither ancient nor modern, that would be me.

BOBBY: Well, tours of the front are now over.

EDDIE: No more war, difficult to grasp.

IFOR: I believe that it is in the theatre that we will find a road back to sanity. We have lost sight of beautiful things. I want to show them all out there that there is an art beyond all hierarchies, machines and the black shadows that pursue us. One day we will all wake up as from an evil dream and the whole world will smile again. If my Ruritanian fantasies have helped, then my work has not all been in vain. And Bobby, Eddie, I realize that I can't go on with this Ruritanian stuff for much longer. Above all, remember that I am an unrepentant sentimentalist, a feeler of feelings, a man of affection. In everything I have ever done, above all else, I have always tried to appeal to the human heart. Bless you Mam! There. Nuff said. More Champagne!

BOBBY: But what about your last show, Ifor, your going-back-to-the-roots one?

IFOR: Not the last one yet.

EDDIE: What's it about, Ifor?

IFOR: Going home. Yes, my last show. 'Lily of the Valley, set in the Vale. A musical romance. Takes place before the First World War. Our hero, a local conductor, David, returns to Wales. Heroine is 'Lily,' or Myfanwy, perhaps, with the sweetest voice in the South. Ricardo Lewis, the villain, local millionaire and bad poet, tries to persuade her to marry him. But Ricardo woos her back with a lovely baccarolle, a duet for both of them at the local eisteddfod, 'Look into my Heart' and she does, and sees she loves only David, and they go to Venice, to enjoy a lavish ballet, before the wedding in St Mark's Cathedral. Think that's enough of that. Got as far as the eisteddfod, but for some reason, couldn't go any farther. Wonder why? To Eddie, who's saved so many talents, including mine.

BOBBY, IFOR: Cheers!

IFOR: To Bobby, who'd saved so many friends, including mine.

EDDIE, IFOR: Cheers!

(ALL toast. FADE LIGHTS)

ACT 2 SCENE 19

(The FLAT. Late night. CLARA'S trumpet (from phonograph) up on well, with the two 'Sandy Wilson' photographs above sofa. ENTER BOBBY, IFOR from theatre below. IFOR clutches chest in pain)

BOBBY: You got ten curtain calls, Ifor. Is there no end to it? Four shows on tour, one long running in the West End. And not one note from your silver trumpet of a tongue on stage but lots of lovely voice.

IFOR: My voice didn't break at Oxford Bobby, it got broken. Vocal muscles tore, permanently. Doctor warned me. Forever the man in the blue suit after that. Something unspoken. Didn't want to burden you.

BOBBY: We all knew…

IFOR: …which is what makes you the best of friends.

BOBBY: You all right?

IFOR: What you need is a glass of Champagne.

(Gets bottle. Strains to take out cork. Gasps, clutches chest. Collapses. BOBBY helps him onto sofa)

IFOR: Bobby, love, I think I've had it.

BOBBY: No, No! *(Telephones)* Stage door? Get a doctor up here at once.

(Rushes back to IFOR. IFOR dying. BOBBY holds IFOR'S hand, strokes it. IFOR points at the trumpet)

BOBBY: Music? Myfanwy? Yes? Why Myfanwy, my love?

IFOR: Myfanwy was my sister. She died after five days. Mam always wanted a girl, a family. Mam, Dad, Myfanwy, me – family.

(As he dies, song Myfanwy played, same voice as at beginning. The song mixes with medley of voices from the past, MAM, DAD, BOBBY, EDDIE, CHARWOMAN, NEWSPAPER VENDORS, KATIE. The 'Sandy Wilson' photos high centre, as at opening scene. Special light effects - fluttering white feathers fill the stage, some change shape into musical notation. Note images thicken, gathering above IFOR. Everything in white. Song begins to fade. BOBBY bows over IFOR's hand kisses it, strokes IFOR'S forehead. Sits bowed. White notes gather, feathers thicken. The NEWSPAPER VENDORS, in black, stand each side of stage, holding papers, sheets all black, heads bowed. FADE LIGHTS, SOUND)

CURTAIN

LOST AND FOUND

A novella - towards a new definition of 'romantic comedy'

by

Dedwydd Jones

Alex looked at the familiar old front door. The panels were cracked and peeling. As ever. From the mortar at the top step bloomed a single glistening yellow ragwort. He stooped down and caressed it. What a pleasant surprise. He plucked it up, sure at least this was a good omen. He noticed the Yale lock was gleaming and new. He carefully inserted the key Marcus had given him and twisted. Success! The door creaked open. Alex peered around. The hallway shared the same neglected look, with junk mail scattered over the loose uncarpeted floorboards. The door he had been directed to should be on the right. Yes, there it was. Marcus had not let him down. This squat was his for the taking. He turned the knob. Success again! He stepped cautiously into the room. He stared with astonishment at the piles of discarded furniture in front of him, old stained mattresses, rickety coffee tables, chairs without legs, sofas with stuffing hanging out, sideboards without drawers, rusting biscuit tins, rolled up rotting mats, piles of tatty curtains, crushed cardboard boxes, pieces of broken crockery, wardrobes without hangers, iron bedsteads all stacked up high to the ceiling. Yes, he thought, surveying the scene, this is more than inadequate for my needs! In the dusty fireplace, inside an old battered pram with a bunch of antique LP's, stood an ancient gramophone. He liked the look of the trumpet rising up from the machine, as if aimed at him, from, it seemed, 'His Master's Voice' itself. Forget the placid dog! Now, he thought, if this is genuine…? He looked closer, no, a replica, but still looking good. He wound it up and tried an old record on the turntable. Lo and behold, above the scratchings and clickings, he was transfixed - the last triumphal whoops and divine blarings of the fourth movement of Beethoven's seventh hove into view. As was his wont, he wept silently, absorbing the beauty up to the sobbing finale, then switched off with a sigh and dried his tears. This gramophone would be his invalide consolation, there in the vacant fireplace, with symphonies intact, and all for free. Good old Marcus. He was sure he had left it there for him. He rescued an old cracked cup from a pile of trash, placed the ragwort in it, and put it on the sill in the bay window, a splash of living colour and resonant tissue. He sat down wearily on the bed.

Yet again he had been walking the streets aimlessly, hefting the heavy pack from side to side, wondering about a job. He had tried every telephone number and address he had. No good. He had only decided to try Marcus's key as a last resort. The squats had often been filled to overflowing, but this time there were no visible comings and goings, and glory be, the key had worked! He got up and peered through a crack in the curtains. They wouldn't find him here. He looked up and down the road. He knew the area well from his visits to get drunk with Marcus and his brief excursions into employment. But so much had changed in so short a time. The old neglected Chatterton Row of houses, born on the wrong side of the river, looked tidied up, freshly painted, the bins in neat lines, except for number 35, of course, the squat which they had christened, 'The Final Frontier.' This haven was the last in the line. Marcus had squatted in the first house, then the second, then the third until the City authorities got fed up with him, but now he was here at the last one and it was all supposed to be "in order and above board!" as Marcus had arranged it. Alex gazed at the cluster of small shops opposite - a Little Gong Café, a Hair Salon, a Toy Shop, a Fish and Chip Emporium, a Wedding Fitters, a Funeral Parlour, a Post Office, second hand bookshop, everything a civilized squatter might need. Next to the shops, on the corner opposite, stood a pub. The swinging sign proclaimed 'The Jolly Waterman.' The adjoining greengrocer's shop offered some hope of nutrient.

He carried on poking around. The panes of the back window were blacked out with white-wash, as if someone had wanted to hide this pathetic junk from the world. On an old iron-framed army cot in the bay window space lay a grungy palliasse half full of bulging foam-rubber. The window was hung with tattered lace curtains with a delicate rose pattern. Ah, thought Alex, not put off in the least by the heavy smell of decay and the dust particles settling down again after his searches. 'A blessed spot, a splendid couch to ease my aching bones. All the comforts of home!' Good old Marcus, a real mate. But where was he?

Alex slipped off his huge army ruck-sack with its iron frame and a thousand straps, the only reminder of his time in the military. It held all his possessions, his manuscripts, precious books, his old school tie, worn when looking for jobs and doing useless interviews. He unrolled his grandfather's nightgown. His grandfather had, in turn, inherited it from his grandfather so the nightgown was at least 150 years old. It was made of the finest flannelette, uncreased after the long years of wear, was light in texture and warm in all weathers. It was the last garment worn by his father and he had made sure that the Funeral Parlour Director had removed it. Now it was his son's and his unto the end too. How it reminded him of his father and the land of his fathers. He stroked it and laid it out on the bed and contemplated his future, which wasn't much. He had sent his emergency request for a job to the tight-arsed Director of the Tourist Tours Centre. Alex knew the City well from guided tours previously done. "Perhaps later," the Director had replied when he had called, "but no forwarding address, no job," he had added with a smirk, no doubt recalling the nasty poem Alex had sent him, "'You are One of These!' By I Watts, adapted by A Parry:

"There are numbers of mankind who creep
Into the world to eat and sleep,
And know no reason why they're born
But merely to consume the corn,
And when they die
There's nothing to be said,
Except they ate up all their bread,
Drank up their drink and went to bed."

Alex fondly remembered sending a photocopy of this to one or two employers who had granted him prolonged early release on grounds of health and beauty! Never mind! Perhaps he should try teaching again. 'English as a foreign Language' it was called and he had enjoyed learning his mother tongue all over again. The English Language was an industry now and Principals could always find students, well under the minimum wage, with no rights, to teach class. Dick Enright, Head of the Anglia School of English, where Alex had worked, was such a one. As a long-standing member of the local Chamber of Commerce, he had decided to join in the English Language bonanza. He had bought an old vacant school building, tarted it up, put up lots of notices, stuck in a business administrator, added an obedient youthful teacher, called him 'Principal,' to ensure his future, and watched the currencies, from yen to euros, come pouring in. But he could never escape his intense dislike of these young unemployed ex-students from good homes, who were at last confronted with the real world, like that cheeky sod Alex, always crawling after him for jobs. He'd show them! Hire them, underpay them, and if they complained, sack them. And he'd never even been to a "Uni." 'Town versus gown?' He'd win every time. The snob adolescents were doomed, however gifted, gilded or decorative. Whatever - necessity called - Alex decided, he'd have to pay a visit to the unqualified shite Enright - the jumped up, nasty, grasping, little upper/lower class piglet, who'd got the foreman's job at last! He'd beard the sod in his den!" He remembered Enright's valedictory insult, what a blight! - "The trouble with you, Alex, is that after looking at you for a while, people always want to throw stones." Yes, and his own riposte, he remembered that well too, it had driven Enright into a blind rage, "You Are One of These…'

But 'no permanent address!' the man had said. He suddenly whooped, for it struck him between the eyes that he **did** now have an address! Let the bastards condescend to their evil spite's content, he now possessed a traceable personality, an official being, a real employable presence, for he had come into the possession of an actual, down-to-earth postal dormitory location, 38 Chatterton Row, thanks to the sainted, now invisible Marcus. Somewhere in all that frantic pedagogical prosperity, there was bound to be a little useful something for himself. It was high summer and the tourists and randy girl students were out and about eying the handsome youthful English tutors, like himself, no doubt. And why not again, it occurred to him, visit the Director of the Local Municipal Theatre, Ted Rowe, as well? He had actually succeeded in getting on well with him, and Ted had paid him for four sketches for the City's last annual Burlesque Revue. The Director had need of 'local' writers to placate the town theatre enthusiasts. The vast majority of theatre goers were of course students. The townees wouldn't barge the offerings of posh, brash, juvenile academic Directors

116

with a touch pole, however brilliant. Alex represented the common man, being out of work, from an obscure family who had apparently, never been near a degree of any kind, and who possessed an indeterminate sort of accent. This man wrote of real shit, ordinary local crap, 'more street urinals' - stuff like that. Very low. Perhaps the salt-of-the-earth hoi-polloi were in need of more man-in the-street toiletries to toff them up a bit. Only one book of short stories had he written, but long or short, it was enough to qualify him as a bit of a local literary character, suitably shabby, a scribbler down on his luck, haunter of stage doors and cadger of drinks, the occasional fugitive guest of reluctant households. On top of that irony, people said that he was good looking and were even envious of him. Alex felt little about it, it didn't make him less broke or famished. One day he decided he would grow up and know what it was to be attractive, but not yet. Too facile, complicated and easy to say, he felt definitely wary about the whole 'looks' thing.

He drooped. Yes, time for a nap. Might mask the hunger. He hoped. He was what had been diagnosed as 'an active sleeper,' that is he hurled himself about in bed when he had his dreams, recurrent or new, and frequently threw himself out of bed and wake up bruised and chilled on the floor in the morning. He had once bashed his forehead on the radiator and had woken with blood all over his face. Another time he had drop-kicked a devilish nocturnal thug waving a Stanley knife but had only succeeded in fracturing his own big toe. He had dragged his bed out so there was a cordon sanitaire around the sleeping area. A few days before he had had a placid sleep episode - his dreams came in all colours, shapes and sizes. On this occasion, he had dreamt he was on the top battlements of Edinburgh Castle and was gazing down over the City. He had stretched out his arms and dived into the glittering night and had flown all the way to Glasgow, taking in all the sights, and had landed safely on the roof of the famous School of Art, although he had never visited Glasgow before. These were OK dreams, the banal ones of no insidious intent. But the more intolerably safe ones were sometimes more infuriating than the demonic ones. He had recently dreamed all night until morning that he was doing the washing up after weeks of waiting by a sink crammed with filthy crockery, plate after plate, he washed, saucer after saucer, cascades of knives, forks and spoons, all carefully sponged and wiped and put away, all damn night long. Too bloody mundane for words, a betrayal of what dreams were supposed to be all about. But now he felt a little gentle doze coming on. He lay back on the bed and dropped away with a contented sigh. But after a second, he began experiencing the usual multiple mirages of intense vividness, of shaded figures and bestiaries come alive. The room was suddenly full of shuffling, snuffling hostiles. In the fireplace a shape was emerging, scurrying to and fro chasing its own tail. The hectic bristling bundle seemed to grow larger and larger until he saw it was a gigantic red-furred fox with snapping teeth and solid shiny gleaming silvery eyes. Its snout sniffed the air, spotted its prey, rose up, swelled like a balloon, and, mouth agape, teeth bared, leapt through the air for Alex 's throat. Alex fell back with a shriek of terror. As he frantically tried to punch off the snarling animal, the fire tray under the mantlepiece exploded outwards, the steel basket full of ashes, struck him across the mouth, shattering his teeth and filling his mouth with grit. He awoke in the shuddering room, lashing out, spitting, and wiping his mouth. He bounced off the bed and stood to attention, like a troop, ready for action. Then saw he was back in full sunlight. Curses!

Another episode and far too early in the day. Had the beast been real, or unreal, an hallucination or was it really one of those interloper urban foxes? And the fireplace showed no signs of habitation. Whatever. He had recovered already. He had recently vowed never to take another pill. No uppers, or downers, or sodium amytal or weed or prescribed chemical crap. Those high days were over. He brushed away the much lowered fear of the fantasy, he hoped, which had been there. He recovered in a trice these days. Fuck the foxes and furies, he lay back on the sumptuous, leaking mattress, with its welcoming bare springs. Yes, he breathed - rest and safety at last. After a while, he decided it was time to unpack his rucksack, a innocuous enough task. He shook out up a sheaf of papers, early drafts of his writings. Yes, these scribbles would do. He glanced at the panto sketch he had been working on. Just two pages, but what stuff - quality! Didn't even need a re-write. This he would press into Ted Rowe's hand when he had the chance. He carefully laid out the contents on the bed, the last domestic bric a brac - a Dresden shepherdess with flock, wrapped in newspapers, left to him a few weeks previously by his dear old Dad. His father had been one of nature's hermits, whom he had respected and loved all his life, and who had faded away like the old soldier he was. Was he really gone? Or just departed? Was his shadow sloping among the gravestones he wrote so lovingly about? Just a hedge historian? Never. A real people's champion, a rounded human being with a natural love for 'the short and simple annals of the poor,' of whom he had written a hundred vignettes. Alex breathed a sigh of relief that nothing had been broken or damaged. But what had happened to Dad's library of rare books, which ranged from mediaeval indentures to diary accounts of the battle of Blenheim, for example, and beyond. Were they indeed now stuffed in some builder's skip. But he dared not go back. They were after him, he was the hunted but he had just found the perfect den. They would not pass! Dear old Dad. He'd have to sell these last loving mini-monuments sometime, to survive. But his Pa had been realistic, too, knowing that his son was following in his footsteps, "they'll be worth something one day," he had promised his beloved only son.

He felt a sharp hunger pang and had a vision of chilled fruit salads under a palm tree by a lagoon. He sat up and looked out from behind the curtains. He examined the greengrocer's shop opposite, in detail. Apart from the usual English cox's pippins and green gages and turnips, there was also more exotic fare, tropical plantains, yellow mangoes, wild figs stacked up on boxes on the pavement, tray upon tray, ready for the plucking. He saw the greengrocer take a cardboard carton from inside the shop, full of bits of bruised and damaged fruit and throw it into the gateway round the back of the shop with the other discarded containers. Alex licked his lips. Yes, rotten maybe, crushed, stinking maybe, certainly thrown out in the cold like himself indeed, but food nevertheless and edible - by God, downrightly so! He hadn't eaten for two days. But, he steeled himself, patience. First, scout out the rest of the unexplored chamber.

His first discovery lay behind a tattered hanging blanket in a corner - a perfectly formed toilet bowl, with a basin as yellow as terminal jaundice. He tried the tap. A gush of fresh brown water splashed over him. Unafraid, he splashed his face into it. Ah, he thought, filthy but cool! He filled the cup with the ragwort. Marcus was right, an over-furnished duplex with a swimming pool! Then he spotted it in the corner. Marcus had mentioned it, a fashionable sea-going luxury vessel to go with it all - a narrow ten-foot ancient dug-out, evidently for a very diminutive native inhabitant of the Late Pliocene Age, no doubt. And, yes, he examined it closely, it was genuine bog oak, black as sin, heavy as the devil, evidently dredged up out of the old Danish Camp river-crossing downstream. He sat inside it, knees up to his chin. He imagined himself paddling down the posh river between the colleges with its upper class punts and dolly debutantes, all pointing at him, a surviving indigene no doubt, gasping with awe and raising their Champagne glasses to him. This was fun a trip, he thought, even though it was on dry land, and him a pauper in a three-thousand year old two-ton canoe, give a pound or two, dreaming his mighty dreams, hoping one day some of them might pay. Yes, he patted the bows, might be worth a penny or two as well, and moving it would be fun. But more safaries first. He approached the rickety sideboard by his bed, and shoved the door with his foot. It swung open. Alex peered inside and shrank back in surprise. Glaring at him was a life-size stone gargoyle head in the shape of a mutant devil, its ears pointed, its nostrils flaring, its mouth agape, fangs at the ready. A perfect 'Robinson,' Alex exclaimed at once, he knew not why, so 'Robinson' became its name. He examined it again. Yes, he as certain of it, this was a refugee from the raving local Christian bigots. He reached out and touched it. Yes, of this world alright! He at once felt a certain fondness for it. Why, the sawn-off battered old article was really just an echo of himself – a displaced person, a loner, an oddity in search of peace and a place to lay his head, a misunderstood innocent, unfairly driven into the dark corners of the world against his will, a searcher after lost chords, like Eden or Avallon or Shangri la, or the echoes of perfection in the fading rose, or the Pastoral, or something, to the one who never gave up or in, who clung on with shredded finger nails through mists and twilights, to his elusive sanity, if that counted as normal, or much, to himself, in fact, born and simple, named as bloody 'Alexander.' He patted the leering head reverently and replaced his new friend, never fiend, back in the safety of its dark little cheesy cubicle. He sniffed, groaned - rubbed his stomach again. God, for food. He would have to go out into the world of the shoplifter soon or die of starvation on the doorstep, to snatch a few rotten tomatoes after dark before the profligate, wasteful greengrocer locked up. But not yet. The books and china were still doing their job, breathing with memories of Dad, still worth 'a penny or two,' and full of the most painful of all the pangs of the universe, piercing, inconsolable grief. He still clung to the precious objects, ravenous or not. And he still had the blessed newly resurrected Ludwig. His foot came down on a loose floorboard. Curious, he bent down and raised it. Underneath were floor joists with thick powdery deposits, lathe and spatterings of ancient plaster. He noticed torn sections of faded old newspapers. He pulled them out, brushed them off, and read:

"Russia. July 6 1908. Duel in St Petersburg. Another fatal duel between members of the St Petersburg aristocracy occurred this morning. Count Nicholas Samarakoff, elder of the two sons of Prince Yusapoff, was shot in an encounter with Count Manteuffel of the Royal Horse Guards. The Count fell at the first fire. Death was instantaneous. Another duel appears imminent between Baron M Markoff and Count N Pergamett, supporters of the previous duelists..." yes, yes, yes...? What had happened? But the rest of the yellowing newssheet had disintegrated. Damn! Who won that second duel? He searched for more fragments. Nothing, except a half-shredded pile evidently left by hungry mice. Damn. He was burning to know – Markoff or Pergamett? Damn. He straightened up. Have to skip this one for a while. Get on with the reconnaissance. 'But I will not give up until I have learned the name of the victor,' he promised himself.

Marcus had told him that every squatter now shared a common room on the first floor. Alex gingerly mounted the creaking, bare stairs to the landing and the first door on the left. The common room was very much like his own, except the furniture was less frequent and much younger. He spotted a fridge. He pulled the door open. Empty. Shook the plastic containers. Not a sausage. The oven next to it was greasy and uncleaned, and, worse, bare again of any kind of nutriment. The slop bucket beside the fridge was congealed with dried gunge, sticky sweet wrappers and coffee stains. He gasped as he spotted a bread bin on the shelf above! He hurriedly opened it. Nothing. He shook it. Not a crumb. He stooped to drink from the tap above the sink, however discoloured, he decided, but the liquid was fresh as milk, although it diminished until it was barely a trickle. He shoved the bloody disappointing bin aside. And lo! At once he knew that that involuntary gesture, however dismissive, had saved him. There before him lay the thick top crust of a white sliced loaf. It had evidently slipped down behind the bin. It was tough as leather, covered with thick furry, green mold. It nearly shattered his teeth when he bit into it, but is was FOOD! As it melted in his mouth, he felt the energy surging through every corpuscle of his body. He chewed and chomped on the musty verdant fodder as if it was caviare at a Russian oligarch's banquet in Chelsea. But as he approached the last fragment, he knew the gnawing pangs would return - but not yet! A brief respite due entirely to a small impulsive, even derisory gesture for which there was no explanation, part of the melodious missing link of good, bad, and odd times. And, at last, he thought, looking around, still chewing like a ruminative llama. He momentarily felt so at home in his shoddy, smelly, sumptuous, wonderful new stables. Splendid! And they, the elusive, deadly, faceless, gangster predators out there, male and female, mythical and mortal, would not find him here in his new arbor, with his mate, the gargoyle 'Robinson,' the rasping bed for rest, dear old Beethoven for ecstasy and an oaken canoe for flight. Never!

He opened the French windows on the far side of the room and stepped out onto a fire-escape. He gazed down the steps to the street. Excellent! Even his own crow's nest! He would be able to spot any exterminators and 'mines dead ahead,' for miles around! At the bottom of the iron fire escape was a small postage-sized garden. It was obscured in waist-high weeds, and was cluttered with tin cans, plastic supermarket bags and piles of kitchen detritus in various stages of decomposition. The whole mess was surrounded by a garden wall five feet high, a formidable barrier, and the weather-beaten back door looked solid enough. He clattered down the steps to the door. He turned the handle. It creaked loudly. Good, he noted, no one could sneak in here unheard. He remembered there was another pub across the street at the back, The Rose and Crown, a pre-war emporium in clean tidy brick, and thirties steel framed windows. Pub at the front, pub at the back. Well served for booze.. Only money needed to patronize either! He returned to the Common Room and at once heard hurried footsteps following him from outside. The French window was violently shoved open and a lean young man of twenty or so, burst in. He looked around, breathing heavily. He was sweaty, athletic, good looking in a dandruff-ad sort of way. His curly, uncombed black hair hung over his shoulders His shirt fashionably striped blue shirt was unbuttoned down the front and his flies gaped open. He was clutching a soiled baseball sweater. He kicked the door shut, looking over his shoulder, "safe here, man."

Alex heard the pseudo American accent with a groan. Another of the new mid-Atlantic brand of would-be Em and Em Emperor disc jockeys.

'Neat,' he said.

"You're Marcus's mate?" Alex nodded.

"Any mate of Marcus's a mate of mine! I'm Harry. My room's first on the landing. You downstairs?"

"Yes, the man in the black canoe."

"Say, I like that, man. Cool. Used to be Patrick's room, but he had to move on. You know Pat?"

"I was drunk most of the times I was here before."

"So was everybody, man. And Marcus told me to tell you, careful of the cops…

"…why, is he in trouble?!"

"Everybody is. Look," he pulled a small poster out of his pocket. "Police Notice. All over the shop. Delivered to every house in the area. Eight rapes, see, all students. See the pic. What dopes. Who can tell anything from that, man?"

A police drawing showed the elusive rapist in a balaclava helmet, with the eyes covered with dark glasses, his body loosely covered with a batman-type cape. Underneath, the description was as brief and loose, "Male, Caucasian, in balaclava, dark eyes, burly build, youthful voice, with a thick Lincoln accent.

Telephone any sightings to local police station. Do not approach assailant, he is armed and dangerous. …"

"What's a 'Lincoln accent?" asked Alex. Harry shrugged and went on, "Seven rapes, all in the Town Centre's students' accommodation, all posh girl students, three of them doing doctorates, the rest MA's, the police are investigating everyone they're so far from finding anyone, so don't be surprised if they stop you in the street, in the pub, in anywhere. Same for everybody. And everybody's reporting they've seen him, must be dozens of rapists in this street alone. Anyway, Marcus said if approached by police, not to run away."

"…how bloody right, because I would have."

"…and would have been arrested."

" Thanks Marcus," he said, looking upwards.

"Yes, a great guy."

They heard sudden another rapid clattering footsteps on the fire escape. A panting disheveled figure burst in, female this time, in her mid-thirties, with a ravaged, used up face, running mascara, flaming dyed red hair, lips glistening with scarlet paint, tight mini skirt, fish-net stockings with holes, blouse hanging open, naked breasts swinging in full view, one hand clutching a pair of black frilly panties, the other an air-line shoulder bag. Without a word, she seized Harry by the arm and dragged him out onto the landing. He cast a last helpless look at Alex, making no effort to stop her. She clutched at his flies as they fell into Harry's room. The door slammed shut.

"Whew, very social, nice meeting you" Alex said out loud, "Yes," he addressed the room, "the fornicators of the world are leaving their calling cards for the new millionaire tenant in the luxurious duplex on the ground floor."

Yes, he felt reassured, here in the real world things were getting back to normal. His head was solidly based in fantasy. He heard cries of ecstasy from the rabid redhead down the corridor. The sound rose and fell like the cries of sea gulls over garbage heaps. "Cool," Harry had said. Well, cool it was but it stank too.

From behind the dull, grey curtains of the French window, he gazed at the pub at the back. He could see the world outside but it couldn't see him! He, Alexander Parry, remained undetected, and only insiders would know the ins and outs of the back and front doors. He noticed an electric kettle on the sink shelf. He filled it and switched on. The red light clicked on. Excellent. Electricity not turned off. Nor the H2O. A promising start. Perhaps the 'squat' was 'legit' after all. There was no tea, but by God he intended to enjoy and nice cuppa hot water. As he sipped, the door to the common room opened and Harry stepped slowly but dramatically inside. He was stripped to the waist, his skin covered with a sheen of sweat. He held up what looked like the last remnants of a striped blue shirt. It hung in tatters in mid air, 'I gotta helluva devil woman in there,' he said.

Harry shook the rags in his hand

"What's that, man?"

"My shirt, man."

"She did that?"

"And more, man."

"I could hear her at the height of her fulfillments."

"Cool, man!" He shook the shredded garment again. "Think this is sumpin? Well, it ain't sumpin. You gotta see my back, man."

He turned. His shoulders and the small of his back were covered with long scratches, some bleeding, as if he'd crawled through a barbed wire entanglement.

"Hot! Man, Hot! I did this." He mimed shagging, "she did that!" he mimed scratching love wounds. His macho ego was reinforced by a vanity so strong it precluded any sense of anything ludicrous or painful in this situation, or any other.

"Hot as hell, man. She works at the back pub. Her old man's the Guvn'or. Fifty if he's a day, kinda out of it for younger women, yeah? Nearly caught us at it. But she stopped him dead! Said she was running away with me. And disappears. 'Running away with **me**!?' Not in a thousand years! Just a lunch-time hump-jump. I mean two minutes to cross the road and one to get stuck in. Ideal, man. Had it out with her old man then. No sweat. Not all shook up. I left. She been waiting and followed me. Had to finish it, the shag, I mean..." Alex glanced outside.

"It's OK, man, no cops!" said Harry.

"Covered your tracks, man, like a panther."

"Cool, man. Like I could tell in a flash just now. You're kinda way out. Like Marcus, only no one's like old Marcus, only he's not old. Man! You don't mess up the melodies of life, the true vibes of existence, man, you get what I mean. Like the rest of us here, tho we have to pay a bit of rent to Helga now, everyone wants to shag her, but she's cagey, man, so watch it. Cash, so the landlord don't give a fuck. Just a tenner. Five minutes from the town centre and fresh vaggies. Great!

Marcus arranged all that. Said you were never short of nooky. But where is the guy?"

"I wonder. But I feel eternally grateful."

"Know what? My fuck bitch. Her old man's an OK guy, really. Had a real heart-to-heart talk in the end, man. Like a house on fire. Like him better than her. He loves Elvis. Got all his records. Listen man, promised to give me booze on the slate. Like respect, man. We got on, man, see, like buddies. He's OK with all of us here."

"But you're banging his wife."

"She just needs a lot of help, that's all. Dig it, man?"

Alex winced, lowered his voice and whispered, "Say, man, could you kinda, sorta... lend me kinda like a ... tenner?"

Harry frowned and moved away. "Crazy dame can't wait, man, I'm busted as you, man. Sorry!" He flapped his torn shirt once in the air and was gone. How to get rid of unwanted guests, thought Alex, it always worked.

He tip-toed downstairs back to his new obscure, retirement refuge. He gazed a moment out of the unwashed window and had an image of a thousand mouldy crusts, however green, growing from the trees on the pavement outside.. He poked despondently among the piled up furniture and empty boxes. Might be a morsel left over somewhere, he thought, a Trafalgar seaman's biscuit, for example, they were often ignored and were known to last for centuries. But no. He waved to the friendly grotesque, Robinson, gave the bog canoe a fond little caress, and sat on the edge of the bed. Yes, he had decided. He wouldn't wait until night fell, which was far too far ahead. He would carry out a grub raid on the fruity tooties over the road right now. He would proceed with the speed of a kingfisher to the boxes at the back, dart in, scoop up the rare ambrosial feast and dart out! He rapidly let himself out of the front door - and was promptly confronted by a gorgeous tall blonde, an Amazon with bulging thighs, vast breast works, a sloping swan's neck, a perfect Madonna-shaped face and eyes as cold as moonshine. Her hands were preternaturally large. They grasped a weighty leather handbag.

"I'm Helga,' she said.

A German accent, Alex noted, very efficient, he'd better keep his mouth shut, as Marcus had advised. She shook the bag.

"Ah," said Alex, this was a pinch, the blasted rent collector.

"So you are new boy?" Alex nodded. "I see you have key," she went on, "I put new lock, so you must pay." Alex smiled his most insincere, dazzling smile. Olga, undeterred, took a lined rental notebook from her bag.

"The rent? Tony told you?" He nodded again, not having the least idea of what she was talking about.

"Well, this one month then. Marcus paid your first rent, OK, but I want it from you next month. You got that?" Alex nodded in relief. "Only ten pounds, but on time and no receipts. Same for all who stay in house." She made a note, "I do this for owner and I get percentage, so you pay up. And no worry 'bout this rapist. I rip balls off!" She put the rent book away. Is Harry in?"

"Yes, but he's fucking his girl friend."

"Don't tell me, Mister" she replied. "Huh! He couldn't fuck the Venus di Milo in heat, not a half inch down there. But, "she looked hard at Alex's crotch, "I might manage you next time, so be there with money in the hand, then we fuck like hens and cockerils all day, OK!" She blew a moist kiss at him, shook her ample titties and was about to disappear inside. Alex had to make at least one move. Looking at her bouncing billies, he said in his finest poetry voice, "there you go again, practicing the sweet rhythms of life." Her lips parted in verbal orgasm. "Yes," she breathed, "Just be there, that's all." And then was gone. Alex relaxed. Helga and her bone crushing thighs were fine with him. He'd got a month's reprieve. And probably a month more for the poetry. Marcus was a fucking God, no doubt of it! He strolled nonchalantly across the road. The greengrocer, he saw, was inside serving customers. He hurried to the rear of the shop. He found himself gazing down at burst tomatoes in all their gory glory, bloody and squashed, mixed with and a few oozing yellowish oranges, blackened bananas and flattened grapes. He noted that none of the expensive tropical fare had been squeezed out of place. He salivated at the pong, and picked up a box.

"What you doin', 'en?" came a voice behind him. Alex casually replaced the box, arranging it neatly. The Greengrocer stared curiously at him, a bag of vegetable refuse in his hand.

"It fell off," said Alex, "I was just passing. Put it back, see. People might fall over it. There. Health and safety. You see. "

He patted the box and moved off. "Cheers."

The baffled hostile greengrocer stared after him. As if I'm the infamous rapist, thought Alex. He walked on towards the bridge, past the pub. He'd give it 'Jolly Waterman!" bloody irony of it! No jollies and watermen all the way! Caught in the act with a cardboard box - a tomato snatch, a banana heist! What crap I do think up. I wish I didn't keep having so many of these ludicrous trains of thought, he thought. But he felt no real angst, just the sharper presence of his growling bowels.

He looked down from the railings of the old Victorian bridge. A polished, newly painted barge was just tying up fore and aft at the quay below. The Captain, in skewed yacht cap, blue polo-necked sweater, bearded like the pard, staggered off the tow path and disappeared into the cabin. He reappeared with a bottle, took a swig, threw a few potted plants into the river, sucked on the bottle until it was empty, then threw that into the waters. Just at that moment, Alex was joined by a second spectator. He was short and spare, with rheumy eyes, and old lined face, the picture of someone who was really at that age which is next to the grave, no doubt about it, regardless of any bitterness. He stood there, tottering a little, trying to keep a straight back, chest out, chin in, surveying the scene as if on parade.

"I see you're a military man, too, sir."

Alex's head stirred. Another one!

"62 Company, Royal Corps of Logistics, Spandau Barracks, Berlin," he replied.

"Royal Lincolns," the man said, "in Lincoln. Depot Battalion scandals overcame us because the CO was gay and pursued all the junior lieutenants. We couldn't hold out. We were posted home because of general drunkenness in the mess and unnatural practices in the ranks."

"They shagged all the mounts in the mule train," observed Alex impartially, "and they were unable to move the ammunition, so the battle was nearly lost, that's what I call a real 'scandal.'"

"I couldn't agree more, sir. Look, sir, I have a collection of campaign medals at home," he went on, "from Iraq to Afghanistan to the North West Passage. Gongs for long service, gongs for raw courage..."

"...all above and beyond the call of duty, no doubt."

"Look, I can prove it. Come and look at my collection. Just over there. Let me prove it to you. Don't worry, I am not the City rapist..."

"...just one thing - who won that last duel, Markoff or Pergamott!"

"That would be on the Russian front, sir, and I was never posted there. Why do you ask?"

"A long shot, that's all."

"I know exactly what you mean, sir. My room, just over there. Please, as old soldiers..."

Why not, thought Alex ? This little raver is as harmless as me in the sunshine of the day and the current waters of time flowing past. They walked together to the little room, all neat and tidy like an army cell. With the curtains drawn he could hardly make out the furniture. In the centre stood a display case lined with collections of medals. "Look," said the man, "I was taken prisoner by the bloody Oudhas. Look at my wrists. See the scars. From the electric shocks. A little incision and then the wire attached to the nerve centre inside the flesh, and then, whizz, whizz, whizz! I screamed, I don't mind telling you... but somehow I've forgotten the agony..."

"...it was another life, another nightmare."

"Damn spot on! Thank you, sir. Long service medal here, the Afghan Star, Empress of India, God bless her! - the MM, military medal and bar, when I was a sergeant,

MC and bar again when I was an officer, battlefield commission, and here the last campaign in Helmand Province, where I received shrapnel to the brain from an improvised roadside device. See the scar on my forehead."

"Thanks for showing me to these. A most brave display."

"As an old soldier, I knew you were, sir."

Alex stiffened. He had spotted an anomaly among the burnished metals.

"Got to go now though."

He saluted the old soldier who smartly returned it and remained as rigid as a granite Gunner on a cenotaph. Alex left the murky little guard room in a state of melancholy confusion. He had noticed the numerals on the medals. They all dated back to the 1st 2nd and 3rd Colonial Afghan wars during the reign of Queen Victoria, 1837, 1878, 1879. All defeats! He walked back to the shelter of his strangled, silent, piled up room. He pricked up his ears. The lovers were silent, probably sleeping it off. Why not? He climbed up to the common room. He looked out at the rear entrances of the houses opposite. No cops or marauders lurking about, no rapists, no bailiffs. Paradise! Any chance of any pickings out the back? He noticed a figure crossing the road. He heard it push open the garden door and slowly mount the fire-escape steps, hesitantly, timidly even. The figure tentatively pushed open the French windows and poked his head in. He was about fifty, with a worried, hang-dog expression. He wore an old grey jacket with stains down the front. His shoes were scuffed and unpolished.

"Sorry, didn't know anyone was here." He came in, looking around. "Hope you don't mind. Looking for a friend. Name's Harry. Seen him, have you?"

"Just moved in myself." He held out his hand. "Alex Parry."

"I'm Roy Smith. I run the pub over there."

"Good business?"

"Yes. No. Not good enough."

"Why not?"

"The Misses. She's run off. Not good enough for her."

"I am sorry to hear that."

"Do you know, I think you mean that. I feel I can talk to you, you've got it, haven't you, you understand."

"'Run off?'"

"What do I do now? I tried everything. Dinner on the river by candlelight, holidays in Blackpool at the illumnations. She had everything she wanted. Even a boy friend. A nice guy. I even gave her the house."

"The house?"

"Our marital domestic residence. Yes. Not enough. I gave her fifty-fifty on the restaurant profits. It was all mine, like the house. No good either. Then she told me about Harry. So when he came to call for her, I had it out with him. Nothing noisy. This morning. No trouble. But he ran off. She followed him. With her holiday bag. Gone. With Harry. Even left a note on our bed. I was so shook up I had a few drinks. Thought you might know where he was. Harry loves her. So do I. Light of my life. Don't know what else to do." He slumped down, tears running down his unshaven cheeks. Alex put an arm round his shoulders. He also had no idea what else to do – but only momentarily.

"Harry's not a bad bloke," the Landlord went on, "younger, of course. Couldn't help hisself either. Got talking. A Spurs supporter. Me too. Nice guy. Really. I gave him a tab. I mean I could see what she liked in him. I don't blame either of them. Just don't know what to do." Alex leaned over him and spoke softly and surely.

"Go back to your pub and get stuck in. Work, work, work! Day and night! Throw a forty-eight hour party for friends and customers. Free booze. Spend savings like crazy. Make it the most popular pub in the neighborhood. Word will soon get around. Get in the oldest juke-box you can get your hands on, a Wurlitzer for example. The best rock and roll. Chuck Berry, Roll Over Beethoven, Little Richard, Great Balls of Fire! Loads of jive. Get an Elvis outfit, try a couple of sideburns. Make them dance. Your pub's well situated. Tons of towns folk around here. You'll be packed out. The ackers will flow in. When your wife sees your success, hears all that music and laughter, she'll come running back, you'll see, she won't want to miss any of that big fun, fun, FUN!"

Roy's expression cleared, he jumped to his feet. "You really think so? Jesus, mate, you're right, I can see it now. Know where the juke box is, got all the discs. Get in extra barrels. Yes, success, music, fun. Get on with it! Right now!" He was a man transformed. "I knew you was somebody the moment I set eyes on you. Ta again mate. Like I got my life back." He embraced Alex. "Never forget this. Come and have a drink and a dance any time, on me. And tell Marcus too, I owe him."

He backed out onto the fire escape, beaming, alert, determined, tears dry; not yet joyous, but despair suspended for a moment in the glow of hope restored, he waved goodbye. Nice little guy, thought Alex, deserves every fillip he gets. He'll make it in spite of the dentata Valkyrie and the Lothario of the Torn Shirt. Alex just knew!

But something was nagging him? What...? But...he went downstairs and rummaged in his capacious knapsack and found his diary. Something was in there. Yes, on Tuesday, he knew that at least, July. Yes. There it was! There was no entry but he knew what it was. How could he have forgotten? An appointment at the City Hospital's Psychiatric Unit. That was it! He was going to have his brains tested. Today was the day. He glanced at his watch. And in one hour! The job hunt would have to wait. His brains came first. He would go as he was, in his khaki camouflage gear, a child of nature and counter insurgency. He gasped, feeling shaky with hunger. He idly wondered about the hospital canteen. Would it be guarded? Would you need an identification pass to get to the food counter? Would a CCTV camera follow him around? But, he paused, whatever they found up there in his fucking cerebellum, he now had a home to return to. And new friends, the mid-Atlantic Harry, the generous re-born Landlord out there somewhere, even the flashing, rending, fish-wife harpy, however high her sexual drive might be, even the grumpy overly suspicious greengrocer! And what about the peering stony good-hearted freak in the cupboard?! A solid mate! All that really meant something already. Well, no one could take them away from him! No one. Never. It was all too asymmetrical, too grandly random.

He kicked his way through the long grass of Jesus Green Park. He would walk to the hospital. It wasn't far.

Although he had been there before, he remembered each step of the way. He recalled his fears. Was frontal lobotomy still in fashion? Were they going to slice off a sample? Or was it electric shock treatment, the dreaded ECT? Why shock treatment if he was already in a state of permanent shock? He passed a group of girl students. It was always a thrill to behold the Continental lovelies, no doubt, in search of the perfect lay. 'Here I am, girls,' he cried out, but knew they would pass him by without a second glance for he did not possess a single article of designer wear on his whole body, or even a suspicion of a stubble, no spiky punk hair, never mind, he trusted his disguise. The army cast offs worked. A twit from the front line. No one paid him any heed. He was safe.

He hurried on, crossed Magdalene Bridge. He paused to look at the lovely sweep of the river, lined with sloping gardens full of carefully tended rose bushes, backing up to to the road, brimming with the perpetual Spring of the City, the old tow path leading into the centre, a tourist spot for the punters and their wives in droves. He sat down at the roots of his favourite conker tree. The sun cast streams of light which glittered on the wind-broken surface of the wavelets and illuminated the foliage with a special uplifting green. A passing figure paused, looked down at Alex, then settled himself down next to him. Here we go again. Alex nodded acceptance. Why not?

The man, lean, unshaven, wore an old mackintosh and carried a folding umbrella. He gazed at the shining stream.

"When you look at that," he gestured at the flowing waters, "it all falls into place, doesn't it?"

"You're right there."

The man held up his umbrella. "I knew I'd be glad when you said that. Light as a feather this brolly. Makes me long for rain. But the little shop where I bought it is closed down now."

He gazed up at the shafts of sunshine. "I suffer from light deprivation."

"You do?"

"I take pills for it."

"What kind of pills?"

"I don't know. I just take them. I see you have a book in your pocket. I had a book once, I bought it in the old second hand bookshop in town, but I don't have the book any longer and the shop's shut up too."

"Why did you buy it?"

"I fell into a terrible depression."

"You take pills for that?"

"No, I'm just going to live in Portugal. Thank you."

"No, thank **you**."

"Where are you going?"

"I'm going to have my brains tested."

"About what?"

"Who won the Markoff/Pergamett duel."

The man leaned down, a tender smile on his face.

"Listen, don't sweat over the small stuff. And remember, everything **is** the small stuff."

Alex felt tremendously reassured. The man put up his umbrella and walked off cheerfully like Charlie Chaplin, in the sunlight along the shining tow-path.

Alex leaned back. He loved his familiars. He dozed off again. At once he had his most horrid recurrent vision, why now? - the fearsome pudenda dentata, the fanged vagina. A whoosh and she was at his ear, a fetid, toxic, membranous, egg-shaped female with blackened teeth, yellow pus-coloured, half-lidded eyes, ginger hair in her armpits and all over her body, and those damnable bulging fish-net stockings again. The monster set her claws into his navel and at once went through the motions of giving him deep fellatio. He cringed, doubled up, trying to strike off the slavering monster who was about to bite off his balls and his solitary, precious prick before mangling what was left of it in her chomping cunt. He made a supreme effort. "Ah!" and succeeded in knocking the beast off his body and kicking it into the water. "Got you," he yelled after the gurgling apparition. "And no pill! You confuse me no longer. Fucking cow." After a few moments, he resumed his walk – proud, victorious, so self-assured - down the long magnificent parade of the Chapels and Colleges, past the Museum and arrived at the huge splendidly Victorian hospital, spacious, ornate and oddly comforting in spite of its self-confident bulk. They could think big in those days, he thought, bless them - I suppose. And there weren't too many casualties either. But the solid portals took the piss out of him as he strolled underneath and he felt flattened once more, like an earth worm under foot on a hard surface. But a soupcon of residual triumph remained and he was whistling cheerfully when he strolled over to the Receptionist's.

"Please don't whistle," she said in a stage whisper, "it can upset the patients."

"OK," he said, "as you say - silence!" and he sedately joined the queue sitting in front of the counter. He listened, unperturbed at first, to the idle chit-chat of the two young trainee nurses next to him.

"I tell you, hebephrenic seizures resemble organic amnestic attacks..."

"...but the frontal lobe syndromes are susceptible to emollients…"

"...electrical stimulation of the seizure-prone points comes first."

"But how much is cryptamnesia responsible for schizophrenic confabulation?"

"Apoplexy of the temporal lobes triggers misogynistic mental diplopia, and reduces equalization to zero, so it's not relevant!"

Alex could bear it no longer.

"Girls," he said quietly, "I feel I must warn you such chatter leads to unfathomable silliness."

"What…?

"You are both falling into an abyss of superficiality," he added, wagging a finger at them. They stared at him in incomprehension. Alex's name was called out. "Will Mr Alexander Parry please go to Dr Leon Helpmann, main Laboratory."

"Bye, bye, girls," he said rising, "and don't do anything silly, OK?"

They gazed at the departing figure.

" 'Don't do anything silly'- I ask you," said the first nurse huffily.

"One of crazy Doctor Helpmann's nut cases," said her friend.

"Needs his brains tested."

"The cheek! Can't tell anyone these days."

"And they still haven't caught that fucking rapist!" added the other.

"They should do their job. After all, it's us, the taxpayers who have to pay."

Alex was surprised when he got to the laboratory, they were ready for him, nutty documents and all. The Doctor's Assistant was already at the apparatus, the ECT machine humming in readiness. She took absolutely no notice of the Doctor's antics throughout the whole proceedings. Dr Helpmann slid over to Alex in his stockinged feet. He was wearing no shoes today. He was in a state of high compulsive delight. He was tall and portly, with thick glasses, bald head and fussy habits. He beamed at the world of the laboratory with obsessive bonhomie. The people in it were endless sources of hilarity, tickled by never-ending comedic routines, the butts of funny stories of a recreational nature. "Do you smoke after intercourse," he questioned rapidly, "I don't know, I've never looked." He gave a wild guffaw, and doubled up. "Whatever," he said, "you've got to laugh." And that was why everybody accepted him, he was a genius at laughter. He steered Alex over to the table. He always had time for Alex. He seemed so unanalyzable, his affliction so rare and rich in humour, so helpless yet so resourceful. Someone who had been hanging on the ropes of truth all his life, and after numerous hammerings, rejections, knock-downs and breakdowns, had bounced back, upsetting every decent person in sight with his renewed blasphemous exposures of the bloody human's nasty id, and "everyone has one," he argued, "not one cunt is exempt."

"Yes," said the good Doctor, "Go on."

"Whatever, Dr Helpmann."

"Just 'Leon' will do, Alex."

The Doc's chest heaved with suppressed laughter. What a mad, glad, hilarious pass. "Life is too important to be taken seriously!" he quoted. Yes? No! Yes!! He clutched the edge of the medicaments tray. His Assistant seemed to be above anything he could throw at her.

"Been taking the pills, Alex?" he asked, with a grin.

"Threw them away."

The doctor seemed more pleased than ever. "Good. We will track down the little imps, Alexander." He used his first name as if he was an old, old friend to whom anything could be said. "We have a new machine here which can scan every known malady or anomaly for miles around. Your friend Marcus set it all up, at his own expense." His shoulder heaved. "Creases me up! Are you still having fits, flits and alarms and things that go bump in the night?"

"Yes."

"Splendid!"

"Seizures?"

"They're not seizures, Doctor, I told you, they're dreams about worms."

"Excellent," chuckled the Doctor, "they are practically toothless, I didn't forget" and ushered Alex into a small bright chamber at the back that Alex hadn't noticed before. The walls were covered with the usual glaring white tiles, even unto the ceiling. The doctor nodded to his Assistant. Her immovable features remained neutral during the whole 'treatment'. The only real emotion she seemed to register was extreme boredom. She positioned him next to a solid, square thick-legged chair straight out of Frankenstein, with a thickly padded back rest, and straps for forearms and neck. A hundred cables led from another machine suspended above them down to a cupped helmet fixed to the back of the chair. With a huge smile, he Doctor motioned for him to sit. Alex looked around in some alarm. He had never been told exactly what this new 'treatment' did or would do to or for him. The doctor slapped his thighs and said, "not the chair! I meant today. You are for the tray, the tray," and laughed so much he almost keeled over. His Assistant remained strictly apart arranging the wires and switches.

"We'll have a heart to heart later over a capucino, after this. But don't worry, as long as you keep having the dreams. Now, my Assistant here will attach the nodes from the helmet to your scalp,' he said, "Smile, dear Miss Trollope," he added, addressing her with a good-natured guffaw. The Assistant bared her teeth in response. Alex shuddered at the remembrance of the pudenda dentata and tried to move away. She pushed him back in the chair, looking more bored than ever.

"There will be about twenty nodes in all and it will take a little time. Like this." He held up a node, parted Alex's hair, placed the node against the bared skin, while his assistant literally glued the node down with glop from a plastic tube. Alex noticed that the lead from his scalp was about six feet long and led, via the cap, to a square metallic machine dotted with buttons and lights, switches and meters with trembling arrows and numbers, situated at the end of the table. These wires in turn were hooked up to the small round table close to the chair. The Doctor gently tugged at the lead. It remained firmly in place. "It goes off instantly," he explained with a giggle. "Who?" asked Alex. "The glue,

I meant, see, tight as a drum," He radiated good nature. Alex glanced at the large round table which stood beside his chair. It was perfectly circular, man-sized, sheathed in white plastic, also with, straps for arms and legs built onto it. The entire table was raised on a single-jointed dog's leg made of metal, again sheathed in plastic. The whole contraption stuck up into the air like an immense ungainly one-legged spider with a huge tray on its head. With the Frankenstein chair and its straps, and the sinister table, by its side, it all looked like some fiendish equipment out of Monsignor Torquemada's place.

"Not to worry," said the Doctor, "we'll have such a good giggle at the next session…" his mobile went off. He listened. "I have a patient in the final stages of delirium tremens," he announced, tittering uncontrollably,' about time! But press on, Nurse, and you too Alexander, always look on the bright side …I will return." He shook Alex by the hand, grabbed his shoes, and rushed off amid an avalanche of chortles.

Alex decided on his usual strategy when there was nothing he could do about anything - to remain mute, motionless and totally obedient - while he fled in his head to exotic faraway places, like Edinburgh or Glasgow. I must look like a monstrous octopus, he thought, but with the tentacles waving from my head. That would frighten the demons inside and outside, he smiled grimly. The Assistant, still without uttering a word, guided him to the table and laid him flat out, like a landed skate on a marble top. When she had finished strapping down his arms, legs and waist, she yawned hugely and casually flicked a switch on the machine. Alex gave a muted yelp of fear. The single-legged table abruptly came to life and spiraled up into the air at speed, ducking and weaving, lights flashing, instruments buzzing. Alex found himself on a nightmare journey on the end of a great dipper gone mad. The table wheeled and dipped, jigged and soared, with himself straining against the straps with every motion. God he prayed, let the leather not break or I'll go flying off into space or smash against the wall like a summer blue-bottle! Then the devil table, unannounced, came to a sudden stop - upside down! He hung there gasping, drooping like old washing on a line. Then the nasty plateau the slowly reversed itself and repeated the whole hellish trajectory all over again. But at the end of the flight this time, the table wound down, the movements more and more gentle and he felt himself falling as softly as a feather into a fur-lined cradle. Then he was on a swaying train, the lulling movements were almost hypnotic. This must be the reward for being such a good boy, he thought, I yelled not once. As the table resumed its former stationary position, he found himself smiling almost pleasurably in his bonds. He had even forgotten, for a second or two, that he was still raging with hunger. The Assistant nodded indifferently, and switched off. She unshackled him and was soon tugging off the nodes, sometimes even ripping the skin, she noted with satisfaction. But the white-tiled silence seemed to suit Alex. He too became even more becalmed. The Assistant glanced curiously at him. The patients were usually gibbering by this time, but this one, she saw, was smiling, and swaying, as to music, was it? And, faster than her, he was plucking off the nodes like primroses off a grassy bank. Obviously far gone in his dementias, she decided. She led him to the door, noting that he didn't try to hold on to her, seeking maternal reassurance as it were, as all these wounded pathetic males usually did. Yes. Very far gone, she concluded. Although Alex never saw her again he felt he had conducted himself cooperatively and with a fair dose of dignity, and the paper work, thanks to Marcus and Leon, was already all in order, the medical reports on the optimistic side and fully signed by the most amiable of the country's physicians. Alex knew he was no was no Vitruvian man, but he understood!

At the desk, brimming with confidence, he couldn't help asking the Receptionist if she had a spare sandwich on her, but she merely grimaced and shook her head. He responded by furiously scratching his scalp. "I can't help it!" he said, "ask Doctor Helpmann."

"What a nut," thought the Receptionist, "but not a rapist and quite good looking." Alex blew her a kiss. "Takes all sorts, I suppose," she thought as she watched him leave.

Alex returned to the Green. His itching head gave place to a vision of Harrod's Hampers, packed with luxury goodies. Surely there must be more luscious, quashed rejects outside the back door by now. In spite of the danger of being spotted, he decided on another day-light raid. His stomach was contracting every second and giving birth to - nothing! He scuffed his feet through the long grass, feeling that there was no end to his deprivations, 'a man of constant sorrow.' His socks of course had been the first to go. Then, job, wife, marriage, rice-puddings, Dad, everything. He looked at the avenues of glorious spreading chestnut trees, the shady nooks in the bushes, the lilac trees beneath, the sheer boskiness of it all, the favourite haunts of shaggers of all ages of the Town at dusk. He had never passed through this area after dark without seeing mounted couples thrusting away in the twilight, like newly formed singular creatures of concentrated everlasting pleasure. 'Let copulation thrive,' he thought and kicked in frustration at the tufted grass. A sudden glint by his right shoe caught his eye. He paused, crouched on his haunches, and parted the grass. He gasped. There, right by his hand lay a pile of scattered cash and two crunched bank notes. "No!" he mouthed silently, not trusting to words, can this be mine, all mine? Is Lady Luck leaning over me, has she relented at last?' He tenderly touched the coins. Real! No dream. He felt the notes, authentic! Yes, the Lady of the Crinkley Greens and her kindly seraphim were there, here, with him. Yes, the heavens were not after all indifferent to his fate, however puny. The lovers had shaken the gold out of their pockets, the greengrocer had taken his profit, now it was his turn! 'My win!' He shouted, 'My Money! And," he cried out to a passing tree, "money from the act of love is pure manna! Thank you, ye shaggers of the universe!" In a second he had scooped up the treasure trove and scuttled away, crouching, as if pursued by hunter-gatherers intent on tearing the coin from his grasp. They would not get it this time. He sat on a distant bench and counted out the money, thirty pounds in notes, and ten in change, riches beyond compare. Farewell green fodder! Without hesitation, he knew exactly what he had to do. Eat next to the sky. Share a table with the thespians in the clouds. He positively galloped to the roof restaurant of the local civic theatre. Here they dispensed well-cooked English fare at prices he could now well afford, thanks to the Lady of Luck. He arrived at the self-service queue, and, almost in a posture of worship, watched his plate being piled high with steak and kidney pie, fluffy mashed potatoes, fried onions in rich thick brown gravy. He sat at the table and ate, his eyes turned heavenwards, his teeth working fast at first, then more and more slowly, each mouthful tastier than the last. He felt the whole world, the world of tribulation, poverty, despair, confabulation, fantasy-reality and amorphousness had faded away forever, defeated by potatoes and gravy. He let the mash slide down his throat, mixing with the gulped gravy and sliced tender kidney. When he had cleared his plate, he went for a second of the same, then a third. After that, a huge plate of apple crumble and custard and a steaming cup of latte. He leaned back, sipping the coffee, pulsating, immovable, with feelings of utter fraternity towards all the citizens of all the nations of all the world, especially cooks. Like them, he had been chosen, even if just for one meal. He closed his eyes and felt himself dozing, floating away on puffed up clouds of cotton wool. No harpies in the underbrush. He was stirred by a gentle shove of the shoulder. He looked up.

"Hey, Alex,' said a distant voice. Alex sat up, 'Hi, Ted,' he said.

"How are you?"

"I'm fine. It's the others."

"Always is." They laughed.

Ted was tall and lean, had a commanding presence but could be opinionated and aggressive, even with the workless. But he was the Civic Theatre Manager, and he **had** bought Alex's sketches for the last annual burlesque Review. They liked each other, no reason why.

"Where you living now?"

"35 Chatterton Row.'

"The bailiffs?"

"Over the hills and far away."

"Set up then?"

"Just moved in my things. I have a postal address for contracts and pay cheques to be sent to. That sort of thing."

He was feeling so cool!

"Any job?"

"Tons on the horizon."

"Some of the stories you sent to the local press were OK."

"OK!"

"The Editor published one."

"He published one quarter of one."

"And then you set about him with a poem…"

"They drank their drink and went to bed."

"That didn't do much for your prospects of promotion, did it?"

"It set me free, just for the nonce, I know that."

"You could make it as an actor, those eyes, that profile…"

"…keep your dirty hands off my nice clean profile."

"You don't care, do you?"

"I do, but not much. Yes, love this coffee. Takes me back to the Land of Lost Serenity!"

"Need to get your brains tested," said Ted.

Alex smiled, "why do people keep on saying that to me today?"

"Why don't you try the town tours again?'

"Too many tourists. And the Director's a cunt."

"Well, the girls are magnificent this year,' said Ted licking his lips, 'take your pick."

" I'm half-expecting something delicious in that line."

"And stop scratching your nut. You got lice or something?"

"Electronic fleas."

" Pardon?"

"You want any re-writes?"

"No, but someone to do the press Releases. Just hack stuff."

"I got a terrific sketch right here and now." He took out the typed sheets.

Mike glanced through them.

"I did get a good write up in the local paper for the last ones."

Damn, thought Ted, this is loco stuff but the local yokels might laugh at it. He paused.

"It's got Adolf Hitler in it," Alex pointed out.

"So I see."

"And Ophelia."

"Interesting,"

"Uncommonly good, I'd say."

"Let me hang onto it. Look come back later. After the matinee. Just a read through – possibly. Or are you too busy?"

"I'll be there."

Alex stumbled out, replete and in employment. Christ, what a day! There was nothing wrong with Little Lady Luck, especially if she's in your pocket, even for a wank! A little luck goes a long way but big luck lasts forever! He cavorted down the tow-path, singing and winking at the passers-by.

He hopped into a little pub he had never visited before. Why not? he was a paying patron now! The building had been converted from a Edwardian family house and looked more like a home than a pub. Alex tentatively pushed open the door. The bar was tiny, just enough room at the counter for a single customer. The landlady appeared. "Half of bitter, please." He wished he could have ordered a quarter of bitter and be more rapidly on his way, for the thin-lipped, sour-faced, overweight Landlady served him with all the alacrity of a decrepit snail. Typical of her, I suppose, he thought.

"And for me please," came a voice behind him. Alex moved out of the way for the next unfortunate customer.

"Cheers," said Alex.

"Cheers."

"First time I ever been in here," Alex volunteered.

"Me too," said the man," I'm a travelling salesman and I needed to fill up. The car, I mean."

"Beautiful day, holiday weather." Alex was determined not to allow any kind of silence to envelope them before he had finished his drink, for any kind of silence would not have been golden.

"You're right. We, the wife and me, always go for a farming holiday in the countryside."

"Really? Where?"

"To Wales, West Pembrokeshre."

Alex felt a cold shiver up his spine.

"Really? Where?"

"Near St David's, booked for two weeks, going next month, a farm, Henllys, I mean, however you say it."

Alex remained fixed to the spot. The man took out his wallet and extracted a photograph.

"Look."

Alex forced himself to look. In the picture was Eirwen, his cousin, and Kenfin, Eirwen's brother, Kenfin's wife and two kids. They were sitting on the bonnet of their old Rover, smiling happily. Alex pointed to Eirwen. "That is my cousin, Eirwen. That is Kenfin, his brother." The man stared at him in some alarm, "How... the devil did you, I mean...I never been in this pub before... I mean, who are you?"

"Their cousin," Alex said. "And by the way, you can't go on your holiday there this year."

"What you....talkin' about? Why not?"

"My cousin Kenfin, there, died two weeks ago, massive cerebral haemorrhage. I was at the funeral. Only forty-four. That is why you can't go on that holiday."

The man backed away, as from a dangerous assailant, his face white. He retreated to the door and was gone.

One of those days, Alex thought, but typical, but I got pennies in my pocket and bread on my plate, so let it all hang out, ye fates and fortunes! He recited the new fiscal tenures of his life, from one to forty, each one worth a pound, as he strolled along under the blue skies and the passing simple clouds. Now he could swagger into the Little Gong for a full breakfast all day, buy top trains at the toy shop – hoot, hoot! Hog fish and chips every lunch, with mushy peas, purchase every royal commemorative stamp in the Post Office, have a lovely shampoo, devour a second hand book before breakfast, ignore the Funeral Parlour Emporium, and the Wedding Fitters, no difference really, and carry home a crate of

Guinness every Sunday from The Jolly Waterman. And these were no delusions of grandeur, these were as plain as a pikestaff in the middle of your face and reflected in your pocket! Mate!

As he passed the gate to the cemetery of the old church, he felt a hand on his shoulder. He started and drew back.

"Ah," said the voice of a stranger, "so sorry" - a plummy upper class accent, "my mistake. Thought you were an old friend of mine, Deighton Aubrey."

"No, I'm not Deighton Aubrey, but I'll keep an eye open for him."

"Thank you so much."

"No, thank **you**."

Thus Alex positively walzed and wondered onward to the Jolly Waterman. He entered, jingling the coin in his purse. He was met by the stony senile indifference of the comatose regulars, sipping their warm beer, telling sad stories about the death of all their cats and yesterdays.

"It's a wonderful day today," Alex remonstrated cheerfully. They seemed to crouch, disappearing into their shells like tortoises threatened by a firebrand.

"Keep on never-minding," he advised them. No? Well, then, half a bitter, please."

Jim, the Landlord served him briskly. He knew Alex previously as an occasional part of the squat across the road, frequently pissed, but educated, he could tell, well spoken, with the traces of a real upper class accent, like his pal, Marcus. Jim was always polite. These idiosyncratic toffs had good contacts. He could always tell, even in these difficult days, who the nobs and who the sods. But treat them all the same and keep the secret intelligence he had on them under the hatches. Jim had a clear view of the whole block through his wide front window and kept on good terms with the tradesmen and postmen in the area. He knew who was there and not there in the whole street, at all times of the day, a mine of information, underhand sex acts all the way, even to the Lord Mayor's chain of office - but Jim was also respected for being the very acne of discretion, which made him a man of distinction in any regard. He was fifty-five, thin as a rake, bald with sharp ferrety eyes and a warm welcoming smile. People were mostly taken in by the smile. The Jolly Waterman was prospering. He nodded pleasantly to Alex.

"I agree, sir. It is a wonderful day." Alex took out his purse. "Needn't, sir. Mr Marcus left enough credit for you to have a few drinks. He said you'd still be in your old army fatigues. I'm to tell you when the credit runs out. I owe Mr Marcus a favour, more than one. Asked me to keep an eye on the house, too, where you live now, I believe, sir."

"God bless Marcus, I say!"

"I agree, sir. But there's police all over the place. Saw them talking to Helga, Landlord's agent, and even she looked a bit nervous. I know they're keeping a watch on the whole block. The Town rapist, I think. But if you've seen the posters, you couldn't tell a rapist from a hole in the ground. Mr Marcus said to have your stuff packed up ready to move on, and the door locked. Cops and crazies all around. Nothing to report yet, sir, thought I'd mention it. "

"My thanks, Landlord."

"'Jim,' sir."

"Thank you, Jim. I'm Alex."

"I know, Alex."

A burly figure joined them at the counter.

"Pint of Guiness, please. Hi, there," came a friendly voice. The man had a thick Irish accent. "I'm Rory, County Cork."

"Hi," Alex liked the friendliness. "Alex, County Sir Penfro."

"You in the squat over there?"

"Ground floor front room, bay window."

"Used to be mine, Alex, but I moved on, bastards were after me."

"You too?"

"Ta, Jim," Rory nodded thoughtfully and took a deep draught

"On me," said Alex, and paid.

"Very decent of ye, many tanks. They think we're all rapists, culling the clever, snootie college girls. I am not a rapist and you aren't too, friend, I can tell by the looks of ye. They've questioned the whole block twice already. Bloody idjits."

"There was two blokes in civvies too, sniffing round last night," said Jim, "and they wasn't CID, either, you can always tell."

"Ta for the info, Jim. I just called in to see if Marcus's back."

"No idea. Floating around like he does."

"Want to pay him back for a loan, thank him before I take off. Back to the old country. Back to see my old granda. His Da was there during the Great Famine, one million dead in the streets, one million gone to America, the rest, to heaven. All the harvests out of the Port of Dublin while my old great great granda died, thin as rake, they said, on his front steps. And no apologies. None. While the corn was shipped out by our nice English Landlords. Genocide it's called these days, got to teach them to say, 'sorry, sorry we were wrong,' that's all. But they just stop and search, stop and search, and plaster your mug-shot all over walls of the world, as if we were in the wrong. What do you do, Alex? Mostly, I mean."

"Try to avoid jobs so I can work."

"So you're a scribe! Good! What do you write?"

Alex reached into his inside pocket, took out a sheaf of papers, selected one, and began reading out. "The Sad Story of poor Rhiannon."

"Rhiannon came from a respectable solicitor's family in the Vale of Glamor, South Wales. Although well-established, the family was noted for the number of its mental defectives. Rhiannon hated them all, normal and abnormal. To her immense relief, some had already killed themselves. Others had been under suicide watch in the local psychiatric clinic for years. Rhiannon worked as a mortuary assistant at the local hospital. Her grandma, described generally by Rhiannon as 'foul-tempered, mean-minded, destructive and full of spite," suddenly became deranged while pregnant with Rhiannon's mother and tried to end her "five-month calvary" with a poker. She was, perforce, taken off to join her relatives in the clinic, where she gave birth.

Rhiannon was said to have inherited all the worst traits of her predecessors. She in turn accused them of "piling vicious hostility upon vicious hostility," and asserted that her situation "only echoed the harmless if-far-from-sympathetic feelings I have held since childhood towards mankind in general," which feelings, she asserted, "given the ghastliness of your typical human, are quite natural after all." Rhiannon admitted she was "unable to endure the sight of happy people" and took pleasure "in placing obstacles wherever possible, in the way of their 'so-called peace and tranquility,'" and went as far as to threaten her more cheerful medical associates with the said poker. Her relations with the patients in the terminal ward was said to be "highly questionable." Further revelations "of a most shocking nature," were later to come to light.

At her trial, Rhiannon was found to be "unbalanced, hateful, hysterical, untruthful, perverse, vengeful and homicidal." When shown the evidence of her crimes, she merely rubbed her eyes and said she was going blind. It was concluded by the Court that Rhiannon's proclaimed persecutions by her colleagues and relatives were delusional and her uncontrollable outbursts, self-induced. The doctors were able to establish that she "had used atropine to simulate eye trouble and that she had forced herself to retain her own urine until she was in a state of febrile excitation similar to that of eaters of opium and smokers of hashish." She insisted she was still a virgin and therefore in a state of permanent innocence. She vehemently denied ever having produced an illegitimate child, another rumour, she insisted, put out by her vile, lying family. Upon examination, her virginity could not be confirmed, which did little to lessen the gravity of the charges against her. She admitted to poisoning "only" nine patients, six of whom had died. She denied any malice, claiming she had merely tried to bring them relief from the suffering caused by the "butchers", that is, the nurses and physicians. Her opinion of the doctors was as low as that of her victims. The doctors were "mad fools," and the terminal cases she had dealt with so compassionately merely "pieces of carrion waiting for the flames of hell." It was subsequently revealed that her string of poison victims had begun as far back as her early thirties when she was finally able to finish her nursing school studies, "emerging," as one fellow-student eye-witness recalled, "from the certificate-awarding ceremony, loudly announcing herself to be "a clinician of genius."

Her first victim at this time had been in a private hospital where the "arrogant, nagging, and immature" Head Nurse had suddenly sickened and died. Subsequent victims, mostly geriatrics, aroused little suspicion for they were on the point of death anyway. But in the summer of her fifth year as a qualified nurse, her victim turned out to be her own daughter. Rhiannon had long upraided this highly suspect and shadowy figure, not only for joining the family unbidden, but for joining in its utterly reprehensive conspiracies as well. After years of suppressed rage at the "barely concealed, unforgivable slanders against me," she decided "her good reputation and professional expertise would never be called into question again." At the height of a hot summer in July, the body of the healthy twenty-year-old girl who lived at Rhiannon's old home, was wheeled out from her sick-bed, and autopsied. After further investigations, Rhiannon was arrested on suspicion of poisoning not only her daughter, but over thirty other persons, all patients, many of whom had died. After the life-sentence imposed by the Chief Justice of Cardiff, Rhiannon was led away, still violently declaring her long-standing innocence. In the morning she was found curled up on the floor of her cell, a beatific smile on her face. She had poisoned herself. No messages or explanations were left behind." Alex paused. "That, Rory, is the sad story of poor Rhiannon."

During the reading, a shocked silence had descended over the room. Alex turned. The clientele had apparently frozen in mid drink for their mouths were still half-open. Consternation was written all over their faces. A few got up and moved through the door like ghosts, with no farewells.

"Well," said Rory, nodding approval, "now that's what I call a story, a real story. The truth. You can breathe it! My thanks, my friend! Now let me give you a few lines of "Dark Rosaleen!"

O my dark Rosaleen,

O my own Rosaleen,

Do not sigh, do not weep,

We are on the ocean green,

We sail along the deep

To give you hope,

And health, and help,

And still more hope,

My own Rosaleen,

My dark Rosaleen.

O the Erne shall run red

With redundance of blood,

'Ere you shall fade,

'Ere you shall die

The Judgment seat

Must first be nigh,

'Ere you can fade,

'Ere you can die,

My own Rosaleen

My dark Rosaleen!

"Wonderful, Rory, I could feel the heart beating in it!"

"And who is this 'dark Rosaleen'?" he went straight on, "You're right! Rosaleen is old Eire, Ireland. We were banned from singing the old rebel songs, so Ireland became 'Rosaleen,' and you could sing to Eire all the live-long day!"

"A fine piece of history, Rory, a fine piece of verse."

Rory nodded, then looked around uneasily. He gestured to the departed patrons. "Alex, there's something fishy about the people round here, and not only the cops, the general population, there really is, so watch it. More of them every day, asking questions, searching your bags. Just watch it. Alex, we poets got to stick together."

They shook hands cheerfully, embraced each other, and Rory went his separate Dark Rosaleen way. Jim hurried in from the other bar.

"Couldn't help hearing, Alex, and Rory is right. People getting very sniffy around here. Watch your back. And your talk was a treat, athough I didn't quite understand all of it. I like something new from time to time, a change from the usual TV chit-chat rubbish."

"You've got a great view of the whole street from here, Jim."

"I do indeed, sir." His sharp eyes caught a movement at the end of the street. "Yes, there she goes, your Helga, at number 25. Got a girl friend there, Natasha, a Ukranian Olympic shot-putter champion, quite famous, writing a book on the history of shot-putting for women. You should see her!"

"No thanks, Jim. I only have eyes for one angel at the moment."

"They're usually the worst, sir."

"Not this one, she has stars at forehead and feet."

"Bring her in, sir, for a drink."

"I haven't met her yet, Jim, but she is in the air, I can hear her charmed wings hurrying near. And thanks, Jim, nice to know you're watching over us."

"Thank you. And Mr Marcus too, sir."

"Just 'Alex' will do."

"'Sir,' is more inconspicuous, for the regulars, so's they know where they stand socially."

"Very civilized of you, Jim."

"Thank you, sir."

Alex suddenly had an urge to get back into the sunshine. He finished his drink and walked along the bank up from the river, surveying the roomy gardens, groomed daily, the roses set out in glowing patterns as on a gigantic majolica serving dish. Out of the corner of his eye he suddenly saw a lithe figure clamber over one of the fences and approach a particularly spectacular rose bush lathered with scarlet blossoms. The figure, an obvious 'she', proceeded to cut off the heaviest stalks and place them in a wicker basket on her arm. Alex quickened his pace. She can't do that to unprotected roses, he thought. God, but close up, she was more beautiful than far off. Just as he would have her, the ideal, he thought, the original maid in Eden, the angel of his El Dorados. Her wings were folded among the roses. She had arrived on time.

"Hey," he shouted, "In spite of your beauty, you can't do that!"

She turned her back on him.

"Please don't!" he pleaded.

"Who're you?" she finally shouted back.

"Let the roses be!"

She pruned more.

"Please don't," he shouted.

"Who're you?" she shouted again.

"I'm a gardener."

"So what?"

"I love flowers!"

"Then say something flowery."

Alex approached her, went down on his knees, and declaimed in his best poetry voice,

"OK! Watermint, burdock, mugwort, and borage, mayweed, mallow, pink campion, Welsh orange poppies, Jack-by-the-hedge, and vervain by mayweed, all in a stretch of ten paces in the midday meadow yonder."

The girl looked down approvingly at him.

"Who are you really?"

"'I am a literalist of the imagination.'"

"I knew it! I knew it!" She was half way to rapture and so was he, "don't ever change!" she urged him.

"OK."

Glancing at him provocatively, she cut another rose.

"Why?" asked Alex, "you can't keep doing that."

"I can," she replied.

"And why?"

"My father owns it all here, I mean, the street, the houses, the gardens."

"You should have told me."

"You are of some interest, too."

She was lovely, short, blond as a daffodil, wide violet blue eyes, beautiful as saucers, a beautiful neck and an air of alertness set off with a bright smile. He body, he could see, aroused his wildest imaginings, in clinging white cotton, little enough underneath – shouldn't be allowed he thought - the perfect garden Venus stood before him, her plump creamy arms holding a basket of purple roses…Never let her go, he thought. Instant action!

"After quite a long chat here, I suggest we go for a walk?" He entreated her, still on his knees. As she was about to reply, a shout reached him from across the road.

"Hey, Alex!"

Alex stood and stared. By the open back door of a chauffeured silver Rolls Royce stood a resplendent figure, beaming at him. The Day of the Cheerful, he thought. He waved vaguely back. Who was this splendid vision of a guy? He was dressed in full Indian tribal finery, like something out of a North West frontier movie. His long tunic, or jama, was of gold shot-silk with embroideries in red, over-stitched with yellow, green and black accents. He wore wide-skirted pants, the remarkable billowing pantaloon with its multitude of pleats. A purple cummerbund kept it in place at the waist. His head was adorned with a glorious jeweled turban, his pagri. Pendants of precious brilliants, rubies, emeralds and pearls, hung from it, a peacock feather upright amid the glittering diamonds at the front. Around his neck were four or five necklaces, of gold and silver, with charms of various gods and emblems of his ancient family. On his feet, bone-coloured leather shoes, shot with silver inlay. Here was a Maharaja indeed. What a spectacle! The vision waved effusively again as if he'd just found a long lost friend.

"Who is **he**?" asked the girl.

"A friend," answered Alex, his mind a blank. He had no memory of him. Who was he indeed? The colourful figure ran across the road and embraced Alex.

"You are my true friend! I knew we would meet again after the Reception. You are a great man, you and Marcus. Give him a message, will you. He, and you, are to be my special guests at my Durbar next month in Registan. All expenses paid. We great ones must stick together."

"I like your wonderful car over there," said Alex admiringly.

"My grandfather, the 15th Maharaja had horse carriage like your gracious Queen, with trappings, harness, reins, saddles, all in antique silver. I have silver Rolls in memory of this! Ah!" he addressed himself to the girl, "You are a credit to the beauty of the entire nation of womanhood, I tell you. Beautiful as the roses you are carrying, but I must add that you are lucky to have such a one as Alexander here!"

"I'm Rosemary," she said, "who are you, if I may ask?"

"Ask many times and the answer will always be the same - I am Maharaja Holkar of Registan, Great King, Samraat, Emperor, Prince Sayo the third, of the blood royal, the seventeenth Maharajah, with love and respect!"

"…and you have 277 pleats in your pantaloons." Alex put in, for some reason.

The Prince nodded, highly pleased. "What a keen remembrance you have, my friend."

"And a great warrior too!" Alex added impulsively.

"So damn right, my friend, you know!! I am the driving force of the Registan people. When I give the order, a hundred tribesmen gallop down from the mountain to die for me! Before breakfast!" he snapped his fingers, "Like that. One order. One charge and a hundred men die - morning, afternoon, breakfast, any time, my young beauty!"

"I'll pass on the message to Marcus, Prince Holkar," promised Alex.

"Just 'Holkar' for friends. I must now go back to my people. They expect it of me."

With his hands raised and clasped together as in prayer, he bowed, hurried across the road, jumped into the back seat, waved again, and disappeared up the street in his noiseless slinky, silver conveyance.

"Your friend is definitely worth 'a hundred dead on the battlefield!'"

"Before breakfast."

"Imagine!" said Roz.

"Alive, like Marcus."

"Who's this 'Marcus?'" she asked.

"A bridegroom in Brigadoon."

"Yes, yes, yes!" Roz squealed again, leaping up and down.

"Down girl, down. Listen, do you realize that there are over 10,000 recorded human facial expressions,"

"Who recorded them?"

"William Shakespeare, everyone agrees."

"I do, too, I do!"

"Just one thing before we go on, you are not in the possession of a fanged vagina, are you?"

"You don't believe that old chestnut, do you?" Her eyes shone with a kindly light.

"Me, Alex," he said, "you…?"

"Me Roz…"

"Short for 'Rosemary. Never change it, my favourite herb, especially in nature, "I know a bank where the wild rosemary blows!""

"I promise!"

"Me, Alex, was about to suggest a promenade through Jesus Green, as the Park is known, then along the tow path, to my rooms for tea and cucumber sandwiches..."

"…I'll just leave these roses for Mrs Clark, one of our tenants, she can't walk far."

She put down the basket next to the rose bush, linked arms with him and together in the sunshine and with the gentle breeze in their faces, walked leisurely down the path to the river and Park. Alex decided to take her directly to his room. Whatever the shock, Alex knew it would make little difference. She knew he was smitten with her, and, he suspected, she with him. Alex took out the key and shoved the door open. He ushered her inside. "My room's here," he said, opened the door and waved her inside. She came to an abrupt halt, looking with astonishment at what seemed like a neglected furniture warehouse. She noted the clear living area by the bay window, the impressive ragweed, and the articles laid out on the palliasse on the sagging bed. She examined the sad clapped out furnishings in front of her with mounting bewilderment.

"Alex, are you on the way up or on the way down?"

"Trouble is, Roz, I don't exactly know what 'up' or 'down' really are."

"I know what you mean, it's alright!"

He gestured. "Here, look, Ludwig, his records in the pram. Fantastic trumpet although it's just a replica. The washbasin, over there, toilets downstairs/upstairs, help yourself, no food, no drink, but I do have my pack of woes and yearnings there. A shepherdess, with little lambs, all in crumpled newspapers, see, diary, socks and stuff, files of writings" He scratched his head. "But now the 'pieces of resistance.' Namely, a pre-historic canoe, a hollowed out oak tree-trunk, located at the fen crossing, the Danish Camp, down the river. I bet you've never seen a boat from the Late Pliocene Age. Don't get in yet. Close your eyes, a surprise. And now…" he took out Robinson, held him out to her, hoping to witness some kind of sweet alarm - "now, open your eyes! Meet Robinson!" "Oh!" she paused in mini transports at the sight, "what a lovely little fellow! And 'Robinson!' a perfect little name for a perfect little gnome." She patted Robinson's head like a pet. Alex was pleasantly taken aback.

"Lovely - this face-to-face meeting is a new experience," she murmured in a motherly way, "they're always so misunderstood, the 'Robinsons' of the world, yet they are always there at holy places to stand guard over us, not to frighten us, but to chase away the bigger demons at our heels!"

"I agree!' Alex affirmed, "gargoyles are a force for good!"

"They are truly benign!" she declared. Alex put Robinson on the mantlepiece. They all beamed at each other.

"Over on the bed," she pointed, "what is that most unexpected garment there?'

"That is a family heirloom, a nightgown of the late Regency period." He shook it out, "the finest flanellete, intact as the day it was born."

"I love flanellette," she said. In a trice she pulled her top over her head, she had no bra underneath and donned the nightgown, which came down to the floor. To crown this erotic display, she slipped off her red, lacy panties and kicked them aside. She smiled at him, "What do you think?"

"I'm with you all the way."

"Good. Let's go for a ride then."

"One thing…" he went over to the pram, "it all works."

He put on the second movement of the Pastoral, tuned it down gently, cast off his clothes, and returned, naked, to Roz.

"I love that 'van' man," she breathed. "Now come inside. Lie back!" "

He snuggled down in the canoe. She pulled the nightgown up to her waist, straddled him, reached down, took his cock firmly in her hand - he groaned ecstatically - and slowly sat down on his erect monster. He gasped as he entered her. God, this was it. She worked herself up and down, from side to side, in and out, round and round, with the occasional suck in between, until perforce, she accelerated and was soon bounding furiously away, timing her thrusts to go with Alex's ecstatic yelps. He watched her amber breasts brushing his own chest and her golden bronzed body as it sped ahead, then slowed down, then collapsed into his arms. Miraculoulsy, they both came at the same time - the elusive 'double O' - and at their very first tryst. The Ludwig music as if in time with the lovers, too, faded to a post orgasmic rest. They lay, breathing contentedly, in unison, inside the womb and vision of their ancient wherry. After a myriad hugs and kissings, Roz slipped out of the boat. She looked down at him.

"That boat is blessed," she sighed.

"Straight out of Avallon."

"It should go home now."

"How'd you mean?" He had a flash vision of the honey dew between her thighs and tried to embrace her. She eluded him and knelt by the side of the blackened mini hulk.

"We must launch it back where it is at home, the river."

"Launch it?"

"Come on, you take that end I'll take this we can cross the road, and take it down the bridge steps, by that old barge, then we launch it."

Alex laughed, "You are splendid," he cried and tried to embrace her again.

"Launch first. Come on!"

"But…" he pointed at his nightgown.

"Don't worry, I'll look after it. And why do you keep scratching your head?"

"Look," he said, parting his hair. "See."

"Oh, my goodness," she murmured, "the glue."

She parted her own hair, "see…"

Alex stared. "So you…too …?"

"…yes. Doctor Helpmann" They embraced.

"But now, Alex, get a grip."

Alex raised up his end of the ship, and led the way out and down the steps. They dragged it together by the bows until they arrived at the bridge. Nobody seemed to take much notice of them, as if they were used to see a young happy handsome couple who had just made love drag a bog oak canoe across the street every day. They slowly slid it down the bridge steps. Although it was weighty, they were able to guide it into its launch position at the stern of the moored barge.

Roz looked over the quay. "Fine! Alex, get the stern, there. Push when I say, OK, as soon as it hits the water, we jump in and paddle it home! One, two, three!"

Both heaved and in a single go it tipped over and splashed into the river. Roz jumped into the floating bows and Alex followed suit.

"I name this vessel…" Alex began. The canoe seemed to settle briefly in the wavelets, then did not stop. "Damn!" Alex pointed, "we're taking water." Water poured in the whole length of the canoe. "Abandon ship!" yelled Alex. They both jumped in and were soon treading water. They watched as the stern rose briefly in the air, then plunged like lead into to the depths. "Damn!" yelled Alex, "come back!" He dived over the spot, again and again but was only able to grip and heave one time. It was useless. The canoe was stuck in the mud like a millstone. He surfaced and looked around for Roz. He heard a shout. In the distance, on the pavement higher up, stood Roz still in the nightgown, streaming with wet. She was laughing so hard she could hardly speak. "See you later!" she finally yelled, pointing homewards, and galloped off, lifting the nightgown so her flashing lovely legs were in full view. By God, what a beauty! "Come back," he shouted, and swam over to the barge. An arm reached down from the stern.

"Take my hand. Go on!"

Alex grasped the hand and was pulled aboard by the Captain, still in his peaked cap and polo-necked navy-blue sweater.

"Damn," said Alex, "that was our honeymoon boat!"

"A most lovely female person," observed the Captain, "worth every penny."

"I agree. Thanks," he looked down at his dripping clothes.

"Soon get dry, put on roof. Take all off. I get drink, come to cabin. I got job first." He disappeared into the hold and was back in a moment, hauling up after him, a dozen flourishing pot plants in pots. The Captain threw them into the water one by one, with an expression of infinite regret on his face. "In case of search," he explained, "Marcus said." Alex stripped off, carefully, carefully hanging onto his purse. The Captain slurred onwards, "and now to prosit! Cheers!"

Well, thought, Alex, my ship has definitely not come in, my woman has run off, and I am left naked in the cabin of a drunken, pot-mad, Dutch Captain, and muck-raker to boot, I bet ..."

"...I am Captain of this vessel," announced the Captain, "I am Dutch and I am drunk."

"I agree. I am Alex. "

"I am writer. I have written best seller, read your Times L.S. I am Jan van der Zwan, a once leader of Free Pot for All. I started free cafe for dope to smoke. And sex on top. I am here, escaped. The authorities want my information, I know who fuck who, and I write it all in public and make fortune out of scandal. Look at barge, nifty, eh, expensive, mine. I wait here. No one find me. Marcus help. What a guy! Got permission. Lotsa police. But fixed it OK. Now, you drink schnaps. Here." He poured out half a glass of the clear aromatic liquid and proffered it. Alex knocked it back with a gulp

"Top, stuff, Jan!"

"That will soon dry old clothes. I like you, so I tell all. Safe here. Forget police."

He grabbed his book and gave Alex an impromptu reading – First, "The Pleasures of Pot," second, "The

Medicinal Advantages of Pot," and last,"The Big Sex Aids of Pot…"

When he had finished, forty minutes later, Alex's clothes were dry. The captain closed the volume, downed his schnaps, saw him safely onto the quay, pressed a copy of 'The Jan van der Zwan handbook of the Revolution of Pot,' on him, embraced him, and gave his invaluable valedictory advice.

"There you go, go fuck her, with pot aaaaand schnaps. Go to it! Give Marcus hug!"

Alex waved goodbye and walked off. O Captain, my Captain! What a genial old genius. And it was true too, he had read the clippings the Captain had showed him, and Jan was there pictured on the terrace of the top pot shop in Amsterdam. No sweat. He patted his purse. There were good times if you kept your eyes open, and your hopes down. It would come, like the Captain! What he needed now, he felt, after all the schnapps, was a hot cuppa char, to get rid of the chills. And to find Roz, gone home no doubt. But, first, a cuppa. He went to the Little Gong round the corner. They also sold cakes and, although he was still replete, he hankered after something sweet. He looked in the window, there was a delicious cream bun on the glass shelf. He went inside to the counter. The sullen, overweight, bored assistant, looked indifferently at him and his sexy uniform, then perked up a bit.

"I'd like to buy that cream bun, please."

"Sorry, run out of cream buns."

"Well, I'll buy the one in the window."

"Sorry, can't sell that one."

"Why not?"

"Because that cream bun is to show that we sell cream buns here."

Alex nodded. 'Do not expect logic from the chambers of the human heart,' was obviously the message of the day – any day, come to that. He paused. Yes, patience and lies. Yes. He gazed fondly at the pudgy face in front of him.

"You look so attractive today." He said abruptly. The girl shivered in delighted surprise. "Sorry, couldn't help it. Must be the hair. Would it be OK to have an eccles bun over there?"

"Of course it's alright to have the eccles bun over there," she returned with a fleshy smile, "sit down, "

"And a cuppa, please?"

"I'll bring it right away."

She poured the tea, got the bun and grabbed a newspaper off the counter. She brought the tray to the table, laid out the eccles and cuppa, stood there and wiggled her hips. "Here's a paper too," she cooed and walked back, casting a come-on look over her shoulder.

Alex polished off the sweet, warming snack and leaned back. She came over and pointed at the newspaper.

"You can take that home with you," she said, arching an eye-brow,

"I've just finished it, thanks."

"Oh, thank you too," she replied huffily and flounced back to the counter. Alex felt a tinge of flatness again, but only a tinge. Shit, he thought, a bit of a blind fool am I, just wanted a bun and a cuppa but end up with a cold shoulder. But never to mind, just watch your mouth next time, he mouthed to himself - and remember, you're a millionaire too, with the most beautiful girl in the world here and now, and although the bog oak canoe has come to grief, you still have Robinson above and Beethoven in the pram below, just two of your new best friends. Formidable! The worm wriggled away. Alex returned to his higgledy-piggledy poet's salon, reinvigorated by himself and all around him. After this mini-miracle debacle, he decided on a little siesta. Then he would start on a Roz hunt. His heart sang when he thought of her and his libido bounded out of the window when he remembered the marvelous bog-oak orgasm and the glory of that heaving golden body. The canoe had certainly moved, and for both of them! As he mounted the steps, he heard the sound of loud rock music. He went upstairs to the common room and peered through the French windows. The Rose and Crown was alive with jiving figures. Barrels had been set up in the front garden, all the widows were open and Alex could see a gigantic juke box going full belt. Amazingly, nearly the entire clientele were in Elvis gear, with little capes, high collars, sideburns, and silvery flares. He heard a noise from the corridor. He turned and went to investigate. He caught Harry with a suitcase creeping down the stairs. He appealed to Alex.

"Don't blame me, man. Look, man, they've gone crazy. That guy, Roy's a real bastard stab-in-the-back, after all. He threw that shindig out there for his fucking faithless stinky gobbling misses, nasty old crow, and guess what? She fell for it. Have a look at her now. She's gone all Gothic, looks like a fackin witch out of halloween, said she'd finally found herself and that although the sex was great, she still had to get to know her inner being. Absolute fuckin' guff! He came over, her old man, bloody Roy. What a geek! You should see him. Wanted me to join in the fun. Even she said it was alright. But they've got it in for me. It's a conspiracy I bet. Force me over the barrel and tuck me to pieces. Yes, there's a lot going on you don't know. So I'm off mate, and you too, if you know what's good for you. Tell Marcus I'm sorry, but I gotta go, and for Christ's sake fuck Helga. She was round here asking after your ass, man. And took my next month's rent too. So watch it, all after you, the City rapist, yes, they believe it, gone bonkers. And the CID are all over, with guys in blue suits. Bonkers. You're a good, guy, all's the pity! Cheers, man."

He gripped his suitcase and was out of the door before Alex could reply. He moved out onto the fire-escape landing to watch the celebrations. Yes, The Rose and Crown was heaving. Yes, things were getting back to normal, but this time in a climactic kind of way, which he enjoyed. A figure detached itself from the crowd of revellers and staggered towards him. It was an apparition of Elvis, or was it Elvis himself!? But there were no vistas of distance or daffodils lonely as a cloud, so he waved back to the gesticulating figure.

"Come and join us, mate!" Elvis roared. He ran over the road, burst into the back garden and rushed up the steps. He embraced Alex and did a little jive on the fire-escape landing. "Elvis owes you his life," he gasped. "You did it. You got the secret. Look, come over whenever you want, it's a two day bash and the cops said it was OK 'cos I got a special private license. And there she is, my misses, together again!"

The misses waved back, the perfect reincarnation of an original Gothic witch, black straggly hair, make up like Nefertiti, miles of mascara, and finger nails as long as ghouls. She looked up and smiled radiantly. It was hideous. Alex fell back.

"OK man, see you later. Dig it. Thanks a mil, again! He rushed over to his nightmare consort and hand in hand they ran back and began jiving on their platforms on the garden table.

Alex returned to his room. Thank God, he breathed, that was a breath of fresh air. On top of his wealth and his status as former sea captain, Parkside millionaire, and restaurateur, he was now a friend of the great, and Elvis topped the list. He winked at Robinson, put on the fourth movement of the Fifth, and lay back on the creaking bed, enjoying a vision of his vision of the divine Roz. At once he felt the familiar wavering super-awareness of everything, in a kind of rippling triple intensity, of everyone he had ever known, the places he had ever been, all shifting like phantasms in a vision of the dark, brilliant other worlds behind the doors. At the same time, he felt the rising half-exultant tug of partial release from his shimmering bonds. Was this the limit of the Final Frontier, the boundary of the Last Mirage? – with Roz at the heart of the matter.

He came to, back to old terra firma, astonished and smiling just a little. The music seemed to be fading into thin air in a most joyous way. He closed his eyes – then started. Two figures definitely sidled round the door and stood there calmly to attention, arms folded. They wore their blue uniforms to awful perfection, their peaked caps under their arms. They stared down impersonally at him. Alex knew the score at once - fucking pen-pushing plodders who would be CID any day now. This was no hallucination, just a haggard, sinking expectation. He put on his poshest accent and looniest cast of eye.

"You chaps like Beethoven, the sixth?" He got up, moved over to re-start Ludwig. "Excuse us, sir, but we have had a report on you and we have to follow it up even if we don't know who placed the complaint in the first place."

"Are you a member of the university, sir," asked Cop Number Two.

"Not of this one, but of a very, very close friend's. But before we go any further, let me introduce you to Robinson here."

"Who, sir?"

"On the mantelpiece here, one of my household gods, the 'penates,' like in The Gladiator."

"Yes, sir, I'm sure."

"Are you in employment, sir?"

"I've only been here a day or two."

"We know exactly how many days you been here, sir."

"Then what is the charge. If there is no charge and this is merely a fishing trip, then let's shake hands and you can go over to the rave across the road, constables welcome, the Landlord said to tell you, eat up all the bread, drink up all the drink and go to bed. OK!"

"The person has communicated with us, sir, and we must add we are keeping an eye on this entire block.

"If you'll permit me, sir, why have you got that fuckin' weed in the window?" demanded the First Cop.

"That is a friendly ragwort, Officer, the national blossom of the Isle of Man, and very medicinal as a poultice for haemorrhoids, may I add, so it might be of interest to you."

The second cop stepped in to save his colleague further embarrassment.

"Do you know of a certain 'Miss Helga'" sir?

"The landlord's agent, you mean?

"An illegal German immigrant, sir."

"Or an Irishman called Rory?"

"Never heard of a 'Rory.'"

"Used to live in this hole, sir."

"We received a report that you were the City rapist, sir."

There was a pause, then Alex burst out laughing. "You should see my psychiatrist," he said, "he's got a bad case of chronic merriment too!"

"Nothing merry about this, sir," said Number One.

"If you know my movements, then you know I have not been here during any

ghastly rape".

"Where were you this morning, sir?"

"Having my brains tested."

"Are you under medication, sir?"

"I merely want to avoid the sad fate of poor Rhiannon."

"Pardon, sir?"

"Ask my doc."

"Is he a member of the university, sir?"

"He is an eminent psyco-analyst well known in the highest political circles in the city and internationally for his famous re-interpretation of dreams."

"Very well, sir."

"We have to investigate every report, however anonymous, sir." added Number two, looking around, "not all of us can afford a proper home, we realize that, but just remember, we're keeping this place under surveillance and that a lot of very decent people in this area support their constabulary one hundred per cent!"

"I am taking all this aboard, officers. And let me particularly congratulate you on your police artist's impression of the criminal. With an image like that, he can't remain at liberty for long. Now let the Master play you out…"

"…thank you for being so understanding, sir."

"And good luck with your life, sir," added Number One "Ta, likewise, and cheers," said Alex as the needle touched the old LP. Ludwig drove out the guardians of public safety in a few seconds and the room reverted to its lumber-like stillness. A busy day, with fewer vistas of distance and pocket-sized Nirvanas, a dawning sense of something near completeness, but still half-imperceptible.

There was a sharp knock at the front door. God, who's this now, he thought? He opened the front door slowly. At once blood rushed to his face and his heart brimful with affection and longing. There stood Roz, an adoring look in her eyes. They gazed at each other for a moment.

"I've brought this, Alex."

She held out a plastic shopping bag. He peeked inside. There lay his granda's nightgown, freshly washed and ironed.

"I couldn't wait to bring it back. I know how you treasure it."

"Come on in, my love."

"No, I can't I've got daddy's car. Got to get it back. I'll be here again in the morning, alright. "

"Wait a minute," he begged. He rushed inside and returned with his special gift for her." He held it out.

"This is for you, Robinson himself."

"But I can't take dear old Robinson."

"You can, he belongs to us both now." She kissed him, hugged Robinson.

"I shall never forget this. Got to go now."

"Just one second again. A long shot, I keep saying. After the death of the son of Prince Yusupoff in a duel, who won the confrontation between their supporters, Markoff or Pergamett?"

"Why, the Czar issued a remonstrance against all duelling in the Duma and the stand off never happened. There was no victor."

"My bright Rosaleen! Another fabulist is born!"

"I'm in my third Year, a degree in European History, I specialize in pre revolutionary Russia and the relationship between the Czar and the Duma. Simple. Not such a long shot. See you tomorrow morning"

Alex watched, slightly dazed, as she retreated slowly down the steps and drove off, waving. That beautiful face, and packed with historical gems! The car, he noticed, was a brand new BMW. Well, he thought, my new historiographer-angel is well housed. He would always be grateful for her ample, timely, word perfect answer. He would count the minutes until tomorrow.

Time to go to the theatre was approaching fast. He was filled with pleasurable anticipation. He always felt he had come home when he found himself in a theatre, although he had often exited with some infamy, stayed on with terror yet still groped there for the truth to set him free. They said his frankness was merely a disguise for scurrility and that he shouldn't pillory people who couldn't answer back because they were so respectable and local. Well, he hoped Adolf Hitler and Ophelia were far away enough from the immediate powers and pillars of society. He decided to wear his clean fatigues and the boots he had on for the launching, although they squeaked and gurgled from time to time. He put on his dried socks with holes as heels and foot mittens for his toes. He glanced through the sketch and found he had memorized it. Just a quick read and Ted already knew it was quality. Alex set out in high spirits thinking over the normal topsey-turvies of the day, and no doldrums either, just the usual - hallucinations, harpies, deadly vixens, un-nameable calms, indefinable shudders, etc, etc. But love, that was no illusion, substantial as the very air, overcoming daily barriers, surviving creeping barrages! He examined the row of houses where Roz lived. All very posh and fashionably running down to the river. Lots of private punts there. He tried to locate the BMW and Roz's house, but no luck. He would have to wait until tomorrow.

He arrived at the Stage door. A message told him to go straight to the Manager's office. He made his way upstairs, noting the stage lights were still on. Strangely, there was a subdued murmur coming from the auditorium. Was it a pre-play party or something. He arrived at Ted's room, who invited him in a most effusive way. A good sign, surely, cash in pocket as well as skit on stage? Ted shook his hand vigorously.

"Great to see ya, Alex, we're all ready, got a few people in, kind of sample audience."

"Thought you said just a 'read through'."

"Just friends. What's the matter with your shoes? They seem to be moulting."

Alex looked down. Sure enough, the soles seemed to be crumbling, leaving a trail of rubber bits and pieces.

"Never mind," he muttered, "let's get on with it."

"Got your script?" asked Ted.

"Know it by heart."

"I'll read Lorenzo the Magnificent and I have you down for Adolf."

"You know the part?"

"Look!"

He pulled back the wardrobe curtains at the back of his office. There stood revealed a gorgeous male costume, from embroidered tunic to curled shoes, from the days of the Florentine Renaissance, and by its side, a portable pawnbroker's sign. Next to it hung the sinister brown shirt from a hanger, so beloved of Adolf, the Sam Brown belt, breeches with jackboots, all decorated with Nazi insignia. A swastika banner stood close by. Ted promptly began changing into his costume.

"Come on, we're on in a few minutes."

"I'm in a good mood today, having eaten my cottage pie and had my wheaten oats, but I am not going into those stupid riding breeches and boots."

"Suit yourself, but those shoes you got on are on their last legs."

He couldn't keep a straight face when Alex had finished costuming himself. "Just great, that's all, a good laff! Come on, let's get on with the show!" He led the way to side stage. As they stood in the wings, Alex again heard the stirrings and murmurings as of an audience.

"Don't worry. Just friends, like I said, Alex. When I give the Nazi salute, march on. I will be there waiting for you."

Ted sloped onto stage, with the pawnbroker sign. There was a spattering of applause. Ted stood centre front and held aloft the sign, "I am the three-balled Lorenzo," he slowly declaimed, with suitable gestures. Loud cheers and guffaws from the audience. He gave the Nazi salute. Alex marched on and stood in typical Adolf pose. Wild cries of outrage came from the front seats.

"Ah, it's you-a, Adolfo, my superman-a! Save us-a from-a da hords-a of da Taliban-a."

"Nein!"

Amid booes and hisses, Alex gave the Nazi salute.

"Christ," he thought, "I am surrounded by people. What is going to happen?" He felt a rising tide of panic. Usually when circled by strangers, his 'enchanted loom', his mind, would go off into paroxysms at the crowded unfamiliarity of it, and spin off into Baltic forests and hide among the savage gods of the Huns, like Thor, in a fine frenzy, after which, comforted by flagons, he was usually carried home by friends, notably Marcus. But this time, as he faced the baying spectators, the panic, if it was panic - or just watered-down anxiety perhaps - he felt nothing but mild irritation, and only at Ted, not the rest of the world, quiet and seemingly forgiving in the wings. But still, Ted, unforgivably, had definitely set him up.

"Are you a member-a of da hords-a, Adolfa?" demanded 'Lorenzo Ted' in a broad Italian accent.

"I **am** ze hords," yelled Alex, in a broad German accent. He'd give them a performance alright!

"I am-a Lorenzo da Magnificenta!"

"You are a termite!"

"I am-a da stara of da renaissance-a!"

"You are toilet paper!"

"I am-a da three-balled-a Lorenzo!"

More cheers and bawdy comments.

"You are **used** toilet paper!"

"No, I am notta the useda toileta paper!"

Alex goose-stepped up and down.

"Leonardo and all his works, ist mine!" he declared.

"Mine-a, all mine-a!"

"Too late! Off to salt mines!"

"God-a bless-a da pre-Raphaelites-a, then!"

"Floating voters vill be shot!"

"Da Mona Lisa, da Virgin-a of da Rocks-a…"

"…zey also vill be shot!"

"Have-a you no-a sense-a of values, Adolf-a?"

"ME!" Alex slammed his foot down. To a surge of laughter, bits of rubber flew in all directions.

"My-a name-a will-a go down-a in-a history-a!" Lorenzo insisted.

"I am history!" riposted Adolf.

"I patronize-a da immortals-a!"

"Immortals ist only me!"

"I'd-a like-a second-a opinionata on dat-a."

"I **am** ze second opinion!"

"Hah, you think-a you got-a all-a da answers, Adolf-a?"

"I **am** ze answer!"

Alex stamped again. A shoe flew off into the audience. Prolonged whoops greeted the flying footwear. Alex, feeling no pain, just a pleasurable feeling of 'I don't give a fuck,' pulled off the other and goose-stepped off stage. Just before he disappeared, he hurled the second shoe at 'Lorenzo' with one word, "Cunt!" The shoe hit its target, to yells of applause and calls for an encore.

Alex ran off, shoeless, down the stairs, out of the stage door and into the street. Make a fool of him in front of strangers, would he, well, that shoe had worked, it had bounced off Lorenzo's fatuous bonce, to cheers, proving Ted's uselessness as an arsehole even, and his, Alex's, high place in the ranks of the top clowns of the Other World, as well as this one. Excellent. He felt no sense of vast perspectives this time, just an overwhelming sense of fairness served and just deserves obtained, and his place in the human hierarchy of idiots at last confirmed. He gave the Nazi salute to every passer-by, but no one seemed unduly alarmed, tho some seemed amused by a shoeless Adolf. Or was it the socks? After all, nothing to fear, the whole population knew of the last days in the Berlin Bunker. He marched on, past Roz's father's houses and gardens, still with no sightings. Closer to home, he heard the sounds of revelry from The Rose at the back, still going like the clappers. Rock and Roll wonderfully splendid. Shrieks and cries of 'Move over Beethoven' and other top hits in that indelible, delectable rhythm! Then across to the Jolly Waterman. He peered inside. He saw Jim who at once urgently beckoned him to come inside.

"Just keeping watch," said Jim, "cops about. Look, just had a mobile chat with our Marcus, what he's up to now is no one's business, tell you later. But one particular guy was here, got your name and all details…"

"…damn! The bailiffs!"

"No. I can tell those swine by the stink. He said it was urgent. So, I talked it over with Marcus on the mobile and he said to go ahead. I made an appointment for you with him at midday tomorrow, a Mr Smythe. Hope it's OK"

"Sure OK. Good old Marcus. Yes. Well thanks, tho God knows who he is."

"But" Jim went on, "I couldn't do anything about the second lot, your old bastards and bruisers, I'm afraid, the fuckin' bailiffs, two of them. Didn't mind mentioning distraints, flits and fines and beatings. Had all the summonses at the ready. They'll be here too. Hope it's OK."

"Yes, fine. Got to face it now. A 'new world,' eh? Sorry, Jim, to burden you with all this. Marcus too. But you should have seen me, the David versus Goliath Cunt stunt! I scalped him!"

"Well, I hope he won't hold it against you."

"**He** set **me** up! Have you seen Roz?"

"Only on the run. Poetry in motion! She'll be waiting for you, don't worry. Go now, here come the flat-foots, patrolling every street tenth time - and talking about feet, get a pair of shoes."

"Trainers OK?"

"And bring your stuff, Marcus said!"

"Right!"

He marched across the road to his front door. The cops didn't even deign to notice him, stupid upper class git student, fackin' Adolf, I ask you, very funny, ha, ha! The Cops entered the pub to enjoy more of Jim's after-party drinks, they'd drunk their fill at Roy's rave already. Good old Jim!

Alex prepared for the next day. He packed his possessions one by one, the books, the mss, the porcelain shepherdess and all her lambs, and especially the nightshirt. Thank goodness he had given Robinson to Roz. He was safely out of the line of fire. He piled the LP records and the gramophone, with its huge immobile mouth, into the pram. He straightened out his sleeping bag, tumbled inside and was off very agreeably in minutes to the sound of - Buddy Holly, was it? The faints, ferments and fears faded. Christ, he suddenly realized that rock an' roll had its medicinal side too. What a discovery! He felt it would remain with him for the rest of his days. And what did it matter if you slipped the slippery traces of life as long as you were commemorated like cousin Kenfin? Mine's a half of bitter, too. Cheers! He drifted off to mundane lands in another recurrent dream - getting lost in familiar territory - and he had no need of spider tables on this flight. The dream started near the college where he had taught for twenty years. How could he get lost there? He was standing at the bus stop outside the old Munitions factory. He saw the electric tram silently approaching, but noticed its number had changed. He jumped on as he usually did, but when he looked through the window found that the entire townscape had metemorphosed, the houses, the shops, the trees even along the edge of the pavement, had all gone missing. Now there were just gigantic piles of rubble, as in Berlin at the end of the War of Towering Charnel Houses. He jumped out at the next stop and clambered onto the roof of the tram to better survey the baffling ruinous architectural anomalies. Where had the bloody college gone? He hung onto the electronic arm of the tram and peered into the distance - just huge smashed buildings stretching up to the clouds, Aztec pyramids heaped endlessly on top of each other, merely made up one pile. When he realized he was in Mexico with the stone snake gods looking down on him, he swore like a prophet, and leapt off the roof of the vehicle into the oncoming traffic. That did the trick and he woke with a start to the scream of tyres. Yes. The usual. He peered into the early mists of the morning. But he had slept terrifically well. He sloughed off the dream like a lizard its tail. Now he had to get on with the day, this time, he realized, to the sounds of police sirens and a chorus of yells from down the street. He pulled on his fatigues and went outside. Apart from the faint sounds of the echoes of rock and roll from The Rose and Crown, there was a louder fracas going on outside number 26, Helga's girl friends' place. As he watched he saw a male figure reeling down the front steps as if from a blow. Helga's girl-friend appeared at the door and hurled herself at the man and threw him onto the pavement. Passers-by promptly set about the struggling, now dazed figure, and pinned him down. Alex glimpsed the head, by God, was it true. A balaclava, and a cape! Was it the Rapist? He waved to

Jim across the road. "It's the rapist," shouted Jim watching from outside, "they've got him." A police car screeched up and Alex saw the figure scooped up off the ground, bundled into the back seat, and sat upon by two solid Constables. Everyone strained to get a glimpse of them as the car sped off, sirens blaring. A second car took the witnesses off to the Station, to make statements, no doubt. Crisis over. No more rape of the doctorates, despoiler of advanced degrees. The runted, stunted deviant working-class sex-snob was now off the streets. In just a few minutes, to Alex's surprise, as he turned away, he saw Helga herself appear from her girl friend's flat, look around furtively, and walk away rapidly in the direction of the town centre. She was carrying a suitcase and an airline shoulder bag. Well, things happening already, thought Alex, but pray, not in my direction. He decided to move out right away. He had a feeling things were definitely impending. He could wait in the Jolly Waterman. He manoevered the pram from his room outside, down the steps, with the master's Voice and LP's and army pack. He was now wearing his old stinky trainers. As he was about to push off, a figure shouted his name and hurried towards him. Hell, it was bloody old Ted.

"Action stations, eh? What's happening?"

"Collared the rapist, looks like."

"Bully for them! Look old friend," he said placatingly, "you know, last night, my fault, but the audience, in fits, they loved it."

"Piss off!"

"Look, sorry I didn't tell you, just a little try-out, not to get you all stirred up like you usually do."

That was true enough, but he felt untouched by it now, sort of whole and cured of it, or something. Jesus, was he over the worst, or was it the best?

"We can put on the show together, you'll be Press officer, to make it pay, OK? "You got Marcus's top recommendation as well! As for the shoe, it just bounced off."

"Think nothing of it then."

"Well?"

"I got a bit of business to do here first."

"Take your time."

"Coming over, later." Alex shouted to Jim. Jim gave the thumbs up and disappeared into the pub. The postman wheeled his bike up to them and handed Alex the mail. "Just one, sir."

"Ta. OK." He said to Ted," I'll see you later today and no funny tricks."

"OK, OK."

"Promise?"

"Promise, Alex. See you!"

Ted mimed the shape of three balls. Alex grinned and gave the Nazi salute. They laughed. Press Officer. Yes, that would give the bailiffs food for thought. They hated publicity! Alex looked up. The morn was breaking, now full of unalloyed sunlight. Alex ripped open the envelope. It was from Director Enright, Anglia School and it announced 'there might be a place, for just a few weeks... just part time at the usual rates, if you would call around…"

"Want to throw stones at me, do they?" He tore up the letter slowly and scattered the pieces into the air.

Sometimes, he reflected, things do happen to go one's way. This was surely one of them. "Eat up your bread, Enright, and go to bed!" he shouted. "Yes!"

He cheerfully pushed Beethoven and all his symphonies over to The Jolly Waterman, this time, His Master's Voice ready with a kiss from St Cecilia.

The first two visitors were already waiting, hidden out of sight in the small adjoining parlour bar. They appeared as soon as Alex pushed open the door. They were dressed like identical twins, two hulks with light blue-striped suits, blue ties, high collars, sleeked down hair, gold-rimmed glasses, small shifty, threatening, eyes devoid of any expression, both carried a black briefcase. They occasionally displayed a phony friendliness to prove their humanitarian feelings and their sorrow for what they were about to do, the sadistic little shites. They wouldn't have lasted five seconds up the Amazon! Alex noted their huge calloused hands. Jim stationed behind the bar, greeted him.

"Here are the two gentlemen I mentioned, Alex." The two stared at Alex, who decided on trying an immediate minor flip. "You want me to tell the truth, right? Well, let me first tell you about the Matses tribe of the Upper Amazon. They have a thing about truth. Among us they are called 'Aphrasiacs,' I am one. They are friends to all literalists too. If they are asked, 'How are you?" they will produce a doctor's certificate to verify the state of their health. If they are asked, "how many wives do you have?" they say "I see one just now, just there, I have not seen another one yet so I cannot tell the truth of that wife or not." Well, if they don't tell the truth like that, they are punished by the witch doctor's curse. They are excoriated but in a devilish nightmare induced by tropical drugs such as the carrion flower, jimson weed, and the physic nut. In the succeeding cauchemar, the liar has to wash his face and hands in unskimmed bronze-coloured water, and, lo! his skin becomes loosened as he rubs, and the epiglottis of both face and hands comes sliding off, till he stands flayed as only a liar can be, exposed to the last pore! 'The fall of a liar is as a fall from the rooftops,' is what I'm getting at, so you can really believe everything I say."

"A truer word was never spoke," interjected Jim loyally.

"All that crap don't wash with us," said the first man.

"And I am now a fully fledged Press Officer, OK?"

"Heard it all before," said his companion. "And what about his nibs here," he asked pointing at Jim.

"He's a friend of the family," said Alex, "highly legalistic as well as possessing a keen sense of observation. He stays. Now, how can I help you?" "Syme and Kind," said the first man in blue, "I am Mr Syme. This is Mr Kind."

"Well," smiled Alex, "not many of us have a hundred men to die for us - before breakfast, so welcome!"

"We are not bailiffs, said Mr Syme indignantly,

"I'm sorry," put in Alex, "I was suffering from a bad case of equalization."

"We are Receivers, we make estimates of all your valuables, from your bank accounts to your bric a brac wrapped in newspapers. Nothing must be secreted. "

The voice was rasping, hectoring, crappy.

"I think you know the situation, Mr Parry. Your former bank manager, your old employer, the local tradesmen, furniture removals and the Funeral Director for your late father and others, are listed here with the amounts outstanding. These you have verified, I believe…"

"…I did not have the money to repay them, so what else could I do?"

"Here are the legal documents, the summonses, re-possessions…"

Mr Syme faded to a halt as the front door was pushed open and another figure stood there. They all stared at each other.

"Good morning Mr Smythe, nice to see you again, " said Jim, "as I explained to you yesterday, Alex, let me introduce Mr Alexander Parry, and Mr Syme and Mr Kind, specialists in re-possession."

"How do you do and who are you?" asked Alex.

The chap remained immovable, giving off an air of something strictly ineffable. He smiled a smile of genuine intent this time, as he surveyed the scene, dressed casually, but not too casual, his dark curls hanging over his shoulders. He too carried a briefcase, but lightly, as if hiding grown-up sweeties. Syme and Kind exchanged suspicious glances. This was too much. Life was a fuck up, mate, a greasy pig, and no one, certainly not this pestiferous swarthy immigrant, the fucking phony arse-licker, was going to screw that up.

"Are you authorized to be here, 'Mr Smythe,' is it?" asked Mr Kind.

"Indeed," answered Mr Smythe kindly.

"Of course he is! - although I don't know who the hell he is," said Alex, "and I do not fucking mind, OK?"

Jim nodded to Mr Smythe. "Explain as you said you would explain to me, sir."

"Yes," said Mr Kind "and it better be good. We're shortly going to take Mr Parry to the Court House where legal aid is waiting for him to give an account of his debts and what he is going to do about it, down to the last farthing, which better be quick."

"I am broke, except for 34 pounds" said Alex. A shiver passed through his whole frame." Thank God it's coming," he gasped out loud, "I waited long enough. Kind of do your best to do your worst. I think you are not giving me a single thrill of fear. It's gone. Hooray!" Syme and Kind stared in astonishment. Were they dealing with an inmate of some sort? That truth shit. Was he round the twist. Could he plead insanity? To Syme's surprise, Mr Smythe joined in, " hooray!" he gently hoorayed..

"Here," said Mr Syme, "you lot trying to be funny?"

"You lot taking the law's name in vain?"

They hunched their shoulders, clenched their fists, shoved official papers into Alex's chest and moved onto him.

"You are hereby served, sir."

"You are coming with us now, sir."

"I think you should listen to Mr Smythe first, gentlemen," said Jim soothingly.

"Why the fuck, Mister fucking Landlord?"

"You wouldn't want to be sacked for losing your employer considerable fees and remunerations now due, would you?"

The pair looked worried.

"What you talking about?"

"How much do the debts come to?" asked Mr Smythe, smiling. The smile seemed to do the trick. Syme and Kind fell back. Syme brushed down Alex's lapels where he had been about to shake him like a rag doll.

"Sorry, sir."

"Just a slip of the pen, I'm sure."

"How much?" demanded Mr Smythe.

"£20,000, give or take a hundred or two."

"Mr Smythe?" said Jim.

"I am a Solicitor and acting as a Solicitor's agent…"

"…who do you represent, Mr Smythe, please be co-operative, like us," pleaded Mr Syme in the falsest of tones.

"I represent the estate of the late Mr Ernest Parry, father of Mr Alexander Parry here present before you. I have verified his identity. There are matters which have just come to light and need to be settled at once."

Syme and Partner nodded in fake, officious approval. "But," said Alex, "my father's will is probated. I saw the accounts."

"This concerns you father's collection of valuable antique books."

"But those were left to the National Library."

"They were not. They were left *in the keeping* of the National Library. The Library contacted me, they held the agreement drawn up by the late Mr Parry and the Custodians of the antique books department. Here is a copy. Note that the collection of books, and manuscripts too, quite specifically, the books to be kept and exhibited for public view during his own lifetime but upon his death to revert to his only son, you Mr Alexander Parry."

"Well, I think we can do business on this basis, sir!" interjected Mr Kind.

Mr Smythe ignored him.

"The key question is, how much are they worth? Isn't it?" said Alex, quivering with excitement as to how far it had already gone. And it wasn't finished.

"Well," urged Mr Syme hoarsely, "how much?"

Mr Smythe drew out papers from his briefcase and consulted his lists, "here, the final total, in the region of £150,000. More by auction, but the National Library has made an offer already for that sum. All you have to do is sign this bill of sale and for me to witness it, with Jim, here, and we are in business. Today is the deadline for the deal."

"Jesus," muttered Alex, swaying, "and I was running away from it!"

"That's fine with us," said Syme "if you could give an undertaking to pay your debts immediately and accompany us to the bank."

"There is no need for that. I have personally guaranteed more than that sum for Mr Parry by our Company, until Mr Parry's own monies, which are considerable, I'm sure you agree, have come through. I have also drawn a cheque book for Mr Parry, which he can utilize at any time. Mr Parry, sir, you are now solvent again!"

"Hooray," he tried, but all that came out was a bemused squeak. In spite of an attack of the shakes, he managed to fill out his first cheque for years and sign his name.

"Now you two, you can drink up your drink and go to bed!"

The bailiffs looked baffled, but accepted the cheque with a bow and a smarmy smile, and issued a receipt. Jim remarked, "I think gentlemen, you can now leave. Mr Syme, Mr Kind"

"Yes, sir," they chorused, snapped their briefcases shut, and bowed their way out of the madhouse.

With a pleased smile, Mr Smythe made his farewells.

"I'll leave these copies with you, sir, and do call in to see us when next in town."

"Hooray!" Alex enunciated weakly, still numb.

"You mean 'hooray!" shouted Jim for him, "with tears of joy."

Alex waved good bye to the second angel from heaven in his recent life! He then turned to Jim, embraced him, "Bless you, bless him, bless Marcus and his ilk!" His voice came back, "Hooooray!!"

At the bar, Jim pulled two pints.

"I am free from the two hooded monsters with thumb-screws at their beck and call. Free as a flying fucking phoenix. I am waiting for it to sink in and it has. I can grasp it without flapping all the way to Glasgow! Hooray! Like that! Cheers, then!"

They drained their glasses solemnly. Jim looked thoughtful. "Our Marcus was in real trouble this morning, Alex."

"How can we help?"

"There's little we can do."

"What has he got himself into this time?"

"He actually helped himself to a war. They never even suspected, dressed as he was in the US Military Police uniform of a Lieutenant Colonel."

"Well, after the failed demonstrations against the Yanks flying in more nuclear warheads, well, he stole the uniform from the Base swimming pool, waited until dark, took a jeep from the officer's mess, and went on an official inspection at the hard hangars where the new J 147, with its special reverse thrust and flap systems, was parked. He managed to get it grounded."

"A blessed miracle again. How?"

"He said he was checking for places where IRA bombs could be cached."

"And they let him in?"

"He had the uniform, the pass, the authority…"

"…the grit, the determination, the conviction, the vision, great! but 'grounded'? How did he manage that?"

"He went to the cockpit with a bursting bladder and pissed all over the instrument panel. They did an inspection, and because of acid damage, cancelled all operations, even compassionate ones, and are now in the process of replacing the entire panel. Cost millions!"

"A stroke of penus! Sorry…"

"…all is forgiven. We are celebrating, remember. And then he simply drove out through the main gates!"

"Absoluely fucking divine!"

The door crashed open and Jan van der Zwan stood there, swaying. He was dripping wet. In his arms was the black bog oak canoe he was dragging along.

"I never give in. So sunk. I dive. So not sunk. Strange soldier on bridge give salute past. Like that. He saluted a few times. "Where I put ship?"

"Outside, with Beethoven," said Alex.

"Of course." He staggered upright, "rapist in cell, Alex, so get to fuck lovely girl quick, OK, so go, go! When you finish, come for drinks and sail in nifty Dutch barge."

Alex saluted, "we'll be there, Captain!"

Jan lurched outside, hauling the drenched canoe. He left it next to the dry pram and sloped off to his pot-free, half-concealed barge on the quay to wait for drinks with his new confreres and allies.

"I was talking over there to the rozzers," said Jim. "Funny how a nice cuppa brings out the real facts… Helga is on their wanted list too."

"No! What for?"

"Fraud," they said. "She stole the rent book from the owner as he lay dying in the hospital where she worked as a nurse part time. He died intestate. She was the original squatter, and encouraged other 'tenants' to join her, collected all the rents, peppercorn, of course, nice little earner, so no one complained, got herself a little flat close by and waited for as long as the gravy train lasted. Then the dead owner's daughter turned up. But Helga's disappeared, they said, only thing left was her girl friend who swears she knows nothing about it. There you are. You have been skillfully defrauded, Alex."

"And didn't cost me a penny. Served my purpose, too. Good old Helga!"

"And Marcus is on their list as well. Only they don't know him by any other name."

"They'll never catch Marcus," said Alex, "even if he'd downed the entire US Air Fleet!"

"Hey," said Jim, "look it's your new girl-friend! He pointed. Alex saw Roz hesitantly approaching the front door of number 35, a local newspaper in her hand. His heart leapt up. He rushed over to her. He held her close and stroked her face, "your eyes are as the eyelids of the new dawn!" She hugged him tight. They looked down the road with a frown at the police standing guard all along the kerb to the end of the street.

"What is going on now, Alex?"

"They've captured the rapist."

"It was on the radio. They said it was the passers-by."

"Them and Helga's girl-friend."

"What are they doing down all over the place now?"

"Closing the stable door."

"And congrats," she said.

"There's things happening and I don't know what they are, Mr Jones. Why, 'congrats'?" Don't tell me you've heard of my miracle, my new job, my late inheritance?"

"Inheritance? don't know anything about that. But in the paper, arts section, first edition. Here. Look! " She held out the local paper, at the right page. She read out, "Last night, before an invited audience, we were at last offered a touch of real satire. Local writer Alex Parry, took the mickey out of the high and the mighty in a sketch which was as funny as it was penetrating. More of this! The Theatre Manager announced that Alex had written sketches for the company before and he was now their new Press Officer. Alex represents a new voice in the town. Keep it up, Alex!"

"I'm damned, and blessed! I mean," said Alex, looking at the clouds, "I am also on the way to fortune, Lady of Luck. I can't understand it, I no longer have to worry about the rent, even if is legal!"

"Don't worry, Alex. But you can't live here.

"I agree! And so do the uniformed officials in the street."

"Daddy's got an unoccupied studio flat, by the garden we met."

"You are the first Rose of Eden and I am your top Gardener!" he sang out.

"Lovely! Lovely! What about this 'inheritance?'"

"Tell you later. Come on, Jim's a real hero in all this. Got it fixed, with Marcus too."

"Must meet this 'Marcus' one day."

"You will."

"Where?"

"At the Durbar, of course!"

"He's all over!" added Jim enthusiastically, "he's just downed a great new bulging U.S. cargo jet, a J 147, a solo flight…"

"…now in hiding, but he'll be out soon, like an imp or a Robinson or the best friend a man ever had, to get up to pretty good stuff again."

"Look," said Roz, "isn't that our antediluvian canoe?"

"Old Jan fished it out and delivered it up to us."

"How kind of him. And your Beethoven gramophone."

"I feel they'll all fit into my new studio flat very well!"

"And I'll fit well into your old nightgown!"

They entered the saloon bar as Jim was just opening the champagne. The wireless was on.

"Greetings, Rose of Tralee! Welcome back, top gardener!" He lowered the volume. "Hear that! Description of the rapist, "About fifty-five, bald as coot, five foot five, scrawny, myopic, a plasterer, out of work, a broad cockney accent," no wonder the passers by were able to hold him down. If Helga's girlfriend had got to him, she would have crushed him flat there and then, like a rotten cucumber. 'Fifty-five,' no wonder the police couldn't track him down." And now they're taking all the credit. It was the passers-by who collared him."

Alex scratched his scalp. Roz reached forward and scratched it for him. They then proceeded to scratch each other's scalps very gently.

"Good to see you doing that," said Jim, "love is not blind. Mutual nit-picking is a sign of love and affection, especially among the chimpanzees."

"Hey," said Rose, "Look!"

To the sound of police sirens, another fleet of vehicles pulled up opposite and threw a cordon around number 35. An armoured car screeched to a halt and a squad of troops in heavy body armour and helmets with visors tumbled out, smashed down the front door and disappeared inside.

"What in the hell is going on now?" asked Alex.

"Leave it to me," said Jim. He went into the back kitchen and emerged a few minutes later with a large tray, on which was a huge metal tea-pot and eight cups of brimming brown tea.

"Our boys at the front need their refreshment."

"No cream buns!"

"Dead right," agreed Jim and went out to the warriors. He offered the tray around. The steaming tea was gratefully accepted and Jim was able to chat amiably to the cops and squaddies. He pointed at the pub, mimed drinking tea. They all nodded and Jim returned to the saloon bar with an empty tray.

"What is up?" asked Alex, agog at Jim's adroitness with the eunuchs.

"Hold onto you hats, folks" said Jim, wrinkling his brows. "It's lucky we're all still here. OK, OK. Yes, they've discovered a cache, an IRA cache of weapons and slabs of Semtex explosive. With detonators. Look they're bringing the stuff out now."

They watched in silence as four troopers from the bomb disposal squad, shuffled out of 35, carrying the material on riot shields. "'Enough to blow up the entire block,' they said," murmured Jim as the cache was loaded into the back of the armoured car. "Where in the hell was it hidden," asked Alex trembling a little. "Front room, your room, under the floorboards under the bed, your bed, in the window space, by your flower." Alex went cold. "It's alright, my love," said Roz pulling him closer to her. "that's why they wanted to interview Rory," Jim went on, "a key member of an IRA cell based in this town." The armoured car drove off, with an escort of screaming police sirens.

"Rory is well away," said Alex, "with the followers of the dark and lovely Rosaleen."

There was the roar of two more dump trucks pulling up outside outside 35. Each carried huge sheets of chipboard. A gang of builders jumped down, unloaded the sheets, measured up the windows and began cutting the chipboard to size. They watched as the gang began nailing up the windows. "Thank God good old Marcus warned us," said Alex, "I got all my stuff out!"

"Look," shouted Roz, pointing. "I do not believe it. Look, it's Dr Helpmann, I tell you, our very own doctor!"

"What in the hell is he doing here?" asked Alex

The Doctor was looking up at the boards, he pointed, then burst out laughing.

"Better get him," said Alex, "before they throw him into the cells too."

He dashed outside. Leon embraced him. The workers, squaddies and cops looked on suspiciously at the two fairy loonies, obviously escapees from the rubber room of the local funny farm. The Doctor pointed at the onlookers, rolled about again amid peals of laughter and began dancing around the lamp posts, as if 'singin' in the rain.' He kept up his prognostic commentary as he bubbled over. "Yes, you said you had an address and you were right, so right. Look, what a door! It's lying down so you can walk straight in. What an obedient convenient portal for a mortal! Thank you, Alex, a jokester supreme, sometimes unaware, but c'est egal! - you were always the most level-headed of all my unbalanced patients."

He performed pirouettes up and down the steps, between the puzzled ranks of the workers and their guardians.

Shouts began to come again from the builders above: "Bleedin' nutter, fuck off, mate!...fackin fairies...shut the row, cunt-heads!...twat-nuts... posh pricks...!'"

Alex held up his hands. "Bless my dark Rosaleen, my own Rosalleen," he sang out to them. The whole gang of workmen paused in mid-curse. "What the fuck now...?"

Reserves of police in their ugly painted greenish-yellow vehicles screeched to a halt outside number 35, disembarked like the plague, and took up positions along the pavement in between the troopers and guardians of the law already there. They looked restlessly at Alex and the Doctor. "Move along, if you please," ordered the Sergeant in charge. "Hey," he called out to the Doctor, "could you move along there, please." But the good doctor continued to sing out his diagnosis as he danced around the lampposts.

"Look, Alex, before the next joke, here," he took a folder out of his pocket. "I have here the print-outs and spread-sheets of all your incredible tests. The findings are quite clear." He flourished an x ray, "you are suffering from a small infarction of the right temporal lobe. The vein distends under emotional pressure in the horn of the ventricule. This stimulates the epileptogenic points on the cortex. Now this gives rise to involuntary memories, preserved or recollected, of otherwhere, a second nirvana, actual segments of a supra dream life, intergalactic transports, random psychomotor convulsions, scriptic illusions, word by word, with illustrations of unimaginable worlds, experiences of lost re-enactments, ferments and exultations even of the olefactory organ, wavering multiverses, leading to the holy swamp-lands of the concrete, ambiguities of the solid state, nostalgias of the future, reminiscences of the world behind the music, this is your universe. This can all be changed with simple lazer treatment, one little burst and that naughty little vein of yours expunged, its influence eradicated, the pressure relieved and the diurnal universe return once again. Now, this little lazer punch, do you want it?"

Alex paused and looked over at Roz watching him out of the pub window. "What do you suffer from, Doctor Helpmann?" he asked.

"But you know what it is!" He slapped his thighs and roared with laughter, which stirred up the builders again. They began spitting at the good doctor and his deranged mate, large gobs of phlegm of which they seemed to have an endless supply.

"Shut the shit up." Splat! "You fackin' nutters!" A big chesty dollop!

"You driveling, spastic, dements!" shouted Alex, "time to knock it off!"

This was greeted with boos and jeers, and more expectoration.

"We are all born in the gutter, but some of us are looking down the drains!" declaimed Leon pointed at them, quivering with glee. The builders looked even more hostile although they had no understanding of what he meant. Those mad fackers didn't speak the same language, they could see that at a glance, and it was enough. But they still did not move on the twin twats. The voices of Alex and Leon were far too posh.

Muttering, the builders went on measuring the sheets and hammering them into place.

"Leon," Alex said aside, "What is it you're suffering from?"

"Alex, I'm suffering from 'Witzelsucht,' the Disease of Levity." He bellowed with laughter by way of illustration. "See what I mean? Why did you choose me as your doctor, you knew of my condition, and why did darling Roz over there make the same choice, or the marvellous Marcus? Lazer treatment, an appointment, Alex? Well?"

"Look at my ragwort there, Leon, still surviving in the window in spite of the wreckers, my bog oak over there, in spite of the fullness of time, my pram, my Symphonies, my unfading rose-love at the pub window there, you, my gifted apothecary here at my side, my new allies, unbeknownst to any single body but me, from Robinson to Ludwig, and I am back with my sainted displaced persons, and I am, nor are they, out of breath quite yet. I think you know my answer."

"God bless you and this cross-eyed lovely dung heap of earth!" Leon shouted joyously, "join the merry gang!" and embraced him.

The builders hammered on, shoring up the windows, blocking out the light, jeering and booing, swinging like Barbary Apes from the scaffolding, exposing their arses the while, making two finger signs and loud fart noises at the upper-fuckin'- class snotties below.

Leon scattered his notes over the pavement, and danced away clutching his head and spinning around the lampposts by one arm, he was singing in the rain and was going to sing in the rain all his life, with fellow refugees laughing all the way to the end. He cavorted in and out of the coppers and squaddies, who were unable to hang onto the elusive sprite before them, until he finally curtsied to the watchers, and disappeared around the corner. An enraged stony stillness fell over the builders, squaddies and coppers.

"Hip hip hooray, the Literalists have the day!" Alex shouted. He pointed at the rapidly disappearing number 35. "The Final Frontier is dead! Long Live the Final Frontier!" He saluted in the direction of the hilarious absent Doctor and strolled back to the pub amid the silence of the wolves. Roz hugged him.

"Brilliant, Alex!!" she exclaimed. "Was Leon alright?"

"In fine fettle. He is someone outstanding."

"What did he say?"

Alex reached out and pressed his finger tips on Roz's scalp.

"Still lots of stuff there."

Roz reached out, "yes, you too."

They embraced again and gently massaged each others' heads. Alex leaned down, "this kiss, Roz, my love, is for the whole world!"

FINIS

ALICE

"Alice…Alice…" From outside the window, the subdued pathetic voice reached me again, "Alice… Alice..." then faded away. I was sitting on 'senior citizen' Daisy Smith's bed in her small room at Happy Sunset Days, the 'old people's care and caring home.' I had been sitting opposite her for over forty years having been her next door neighbour for all of that slow and speedy time. Now she was dying in her room at 'the ever-young residence for the aged' as another of the highly coloured brochures proclaimed. Daisy had finally given in and sold up. She was now far from the little deserted for-sale terraced house on the outskirts of town. Mr Smith, good old Alec, had long since departed. She had a photo of them on their fiftieth wedding anniversary on the table by her bed. She said good morning and goodnight to her husband every day. Daisy knew she only had two years here for the fees were astronomical and she was a prompt payer. Daisy was frail and losing the use of her legs, but she remained a naturally cheerful soul and her remarkably unlined face was full of life. She sat in the adjustable hospital chair which she had to be lowered into every morning. She often talked about her 'condition' but always with a smile. She chatted endlessly to visitors, then to the birds outside her window when the visitors had gone, treating them all the same - kindly friends who'd come to say hello and keep her company - angels. She flexed her fingers and shook out the knitting on her lap. She winced. Nearly every joint was swollen with arthritis.

"Josh," she said matter-of-factly, "tell your dear daughter that I won't be able to knit any more cardigans for her little boy, too fiddly for my hands now. I can still do scarves though, nice and straight!" She addressed herself firmly, "Come on Daisy Smith, not so lamely now. Get on with it!" The knitting needles clicked up and down, but much more slowly now.

"Alice...Alice..." the melancholy voice seemed to rise from the rose bushes outside, not a cry for help, or even of complaint, just a mild whispered plea, "Alice, Alice..."

"Did you hear that?" I asked, but Daisy just carried on knitting. She was going deaf but the voice seemed loud enough

"Look at my legs," she said, raising them up. They were swollen at the ankles to twice the normal size, "but, " she went on," I still managed to go for a walk yesterday, from the Tesco Car Park, with a little help from my friends of course. Not on my last legs yet." She chuckled, "you see, I fancied a nice ham sandwich. I thought I'd buy one of those heart-shaped tins, with jelly, always so tasty and Alec loved them too. Well, when I got back, I buttered two slices and opened the tin. But ugh! Disgusting! All grey, slimy, runny. Just goo. All gristle, and I hate gristle. And the pong! Well, I decided there and then, I was not going to stand for it. I put that stinking tin into a casserole with the lid on. I rang for a taxi and for the helper. I insisted! Back at the store I said to the lady at the customer counter, Daphne's her name, always helpful - look at this, I said! And whipped off the cover. " Daphne did like me - stepped back, holding her nose. "Disgusting! " she said. "You would have done that too, I mean, brought it back, yes?" I asked. "I definitely would have, don't you worry!" she said. "Can I have my money back then?" I asked. "You certainly can," she said, opened the till, gave me the money there and then. "Ugh!" she said again and hurried off. "Come back for the casserole, I'll wash it." She shouted, always so helpful. Well, they all said I was right, Alec too." She waved at the photo. "Not my last walk to Tesco's, I can tell you. Not going to put up with that kind of nonsense any longer, no!"

"Alice, Alice…" again from outside.

"You must have heard that, Daisy?"

She nodded, "oh, yes." She cocked her head to one side. "That's old Fred."

"…old Fred?"

"Yes, so sad."

"Why?"

"He can't stand it here any longer."

"Why not?"

"It's Alice."

"Who's Alice?

"Alice is his bike."

"His bike?"

"His favourite."

"Alice Alice…" came again.

"Why's he keep saying that?"

"It's his mother's name."

"His mother's…?"

"It was his mother's bike. He had it after she died."

" … she died …?"

213

"A lady's bike, with a low cross-bar."

"Alice…Alice…"

"There he goes again. Why?"

"Alice got stolen. He left it outside, just for a minute, he said, and someone stole it."

"Can't he buy a new one?"

"It was hers, Alice's, you see. Yes, all rusty and wobbly, but Fred loved it. Police said it was in the dark and the thieves couldn't see it was old and worthless, probably "threw it into the river with the others, to hide the evidence." Can you imagine! Poor Fred burst into tears when the Sergeant said that and ran out into the street shouting, "Alice! Alice!" and went off searching for her. Well, the nurses rushed after him, brought him back to his room. When they tried to talk to him, he just sat on the edge of his bed, staring, muttering her name again and again. But the nurses were good, they couldn't blame him."

I left Daisy with the doleful "Alice…" still echoing in my ears.

On my next visit, Daisy greeted me from her chair. I saw her legs were tightly wrapped in a blanket.

"Looks like it might have been my last walk after all," she said with a chuckle, "but that disgusting ham! I did right! Everyone said so. Alec too." She motioned to the wedding picture. "Woke this morning, Josh," she went on, "and couldn't even get into the harness. Imagine, we've been neighbours for over forty years and it's come to that. Daft!"

I glanced uneasily towards the window. What to say?

"How's old Fred today?"

"He's been took off."

"Took off?"

"Last Monday. He died. Couldn't hold anything down. Sick as a dog. Every day. All day, all night. Thin as a rake. Just kept saying "Alice…Alice…" all the time. He couldn't get over it. The loss of his bike. Couldn't live without his Alice. It was grief, you see, it was grief that did for him."

"Alice…Alice…" I whispered involuntarily.

She smiled, "yes..." she reached for her knitting, "…yes, we were all sorry, very, very sorry."

END

Titles from Creative Print Publishing Ltd

Fiction

The Shadow Line & The Secret Sharer   Joseph Conrad
ISBN 978-0-9568535-0-9

Kristina's Destiny   Diana Daneri
ISBN 978-0-9568535-1-6

Andrew's Destiny   Diana Daneri
ISBN 978-0-9568535-2-3

To Hold A Storm   Chris Green
ISBN 978-0-9568535-3-0

Ten Best Short Stories of 2011   Various
ISBN 978-0-9568535-5-4

The Lincoln Letter   Gretchen Elhassani
ISBN 978-0-9568535-4-7

Dying to Live   Katie L. Thompson
ISBN 978-0-9568535-7-8

Keeping Karma   Louise Reid
ISBN 978-0-9568535-6-1

Escape to the Country   Patsy Collins
ISBN 978-0-9568535-8-5

Lindsey's Destiny   Diana Daneri
ISBN 978-0-9568535-9-2

Nonfiction

Amazonia – My Journey Into The Unknown - Adam Wikierski
ISBN 978-1-909049-00-0

Contacting Creative Print Publishing Ltd

w: http://www.creativeprintpublishing.com
e: info@creativeprintpublishing.com
t: +44 (0)845 868 8430

Creative Print Publishing Limited
17 George Street
Milnsbridge
Huddersfield
HD3 4JD
United Kingdom

Lightning Source UK Ltd.
Milton Keynes UK
UKOW06f0902160815

256879UK00005B/4/P